Missionary Land Rover climbs newly bull-dozed road in the Jeh tribes country, near Dak Rotah.

D0921622

LINCOLN CHRISTIAN COLLEGE AND SEMINARY

WAGGONER CHRISTIAN CHURCH

VICTORY IN VIET NAM

WAGGONER CHRISTIAN CHURCH

VICTORY
IN
VIET NAM

by Mrs. Gordon H. Smith

Author of *GONGS IN THE NIGHT* and
FARTHER INTO THE NIGHT

ZONDERVAN PUBLISHING HOUSE
GRAND RAPIDS   MICHIGAN

VICTORY IN VIET NAM
Copyright 1965 by
Zondervan Publishing House
Grand Rapids, Michigan

Library of Congress Catalog Card Number 64-8838

Printed in the United States of America

▶ Contents ◀

1. The New Challenge 9
2. Survey 13
3. The Katu 18
4. Digging In 27
5. Meet Chesty and Hopalong 32
6. The Cua 36
7. The Hrey 47
8. Headquarters and Bible School 58
9. By Motor Boat to the Katu 66
10. The Pakoh and Baru 80
11. Forging Ahead 90
12. Les, the Hunter 101
13. Leprosy 108
14. Phuoc Son, Center Number Nine 115
15. The Worldwide Evangelization Crusade 122
16. Seven New Stations 130
17. Jungle Beach-heads 136
18. Establishing Work in Kontum Province 150
19. Preacher Buried Alive 162
20. Tragedy at Dak Rotah 170
21. First Attack on Tra Bong 179
22. We Build a Boat 182
23. Orphans! 196
24. Battles 209
25. The Hreys Turn to Christ 220
26. "Happy Haven" Leprosarium Underway 232
27. Keeping Up the Pace 237
Epilogue 242

119362

VICTORY IN VIET NAM

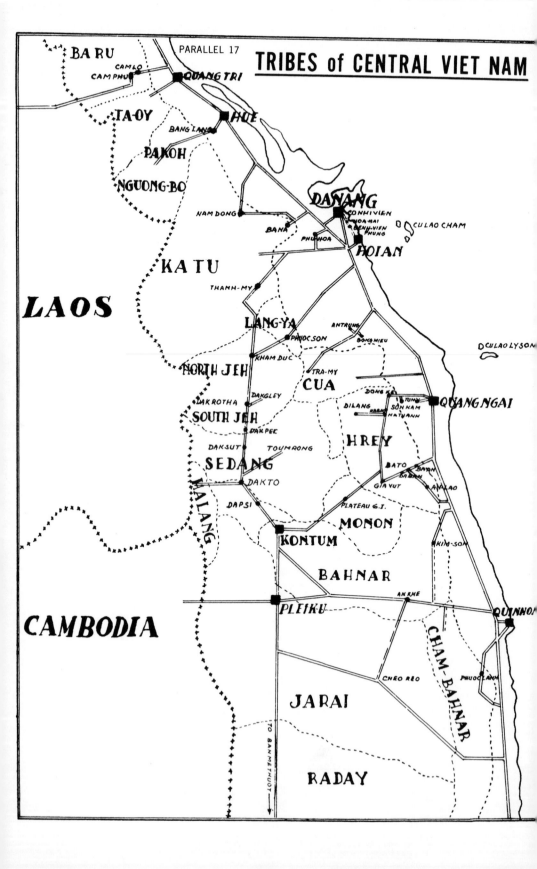

▶ 1 ◀

The New Challenge

IN 1956 MY HUSBAND, Gordon, and I returned from furlough in the United States to Viet Nam, this time independently, to turn our whole attention to Central Viet Nam and the many unreached tribes there.

Our deep and abiding desire to see the Central Viet Nam tribes evangelized, no matter how much Satan would oppose us, was proof, we felt, that God intended us to enter these new, open doors, and in humility, faith and utter dependence upon Him we began to undertake this mission.

We had worked since 1929 in this country — for four years in Cambodia and then for twenty-two years in South Viet Nam, as pioneer missionaries to the tribes. We had labored in hope, sorrow and love, shedding tears and our very lifeblood to plough up and cultivate the Banmethuot portion of Christ's vineyard.

We were now over 50 years old, but we wanted to give the rest of our lives to carrying the message of salvation to the vast outlying regions yet untouched in Central Viet Nam — out beyond trail's end. We would take the cross into these unknown, unexplored regions, walking in the footprints of our Captain Christ. A great gladness and a great humility possessed us. Continuing in the Great Commission, we wanted to be pathfinders and to blaze new trails.

Gordon and I had first visited some of these tribes in Central Viet Nam back in 1937 — going to the Jeh and Sedang, north of Pleiku; and then in 1940 visiting the Katu tribe, wild and unsubdued, near Da Nang, and the Baru tribe west of Quang Tri.

Then the Japanese war came in 1941, followed by the Viet

Left: A painting by a Vietnamese artist. "What crying need is shown in this face!"

Below: Lang Ya tribespeople listen to the story of Christ presented via the picture roll.

Minh Communist war with the French from 1945, and the doors were closed to missionaries among these tribes. We had never ceased to pray that some day "the gates of brass and bars of iron" holding these tribes in darkness, would be broken open and we would be permitted to enter with the Gospel.

The cease-fire came at last when the Geneva Treaty was signed in 1954, and now the door was open to enter these new tribes. They inhabit the mountains south of the 17th Parallel, west of the cities of Quang Tri, Hue, Da Nang, Quang Ngai, and Quinhon. The country was now safe enough to travel into these valleys and mountains to make a big survey and to begin the establishing of mission stations in these areas. The new doors beckoned to adventures for Christ and the souls of men.

All of these great unreached areas of primitive, semi-savage, loin-cloth tribespeople in the heart of Viet Nam, from north of Pleiku, were accessible from the coast by roads that wound into the interior. And we could also reach large untouched sections of tens of thousands of backwoods Vietnamese in these Central Viet Nam provinces. Ours was to be a major missionary advance.

Ours would be a pioneer work among these new tribes of people "lost beyond the ranges," waiting to hear of the Saviour. They were practically unknown mountain people, deep in the black-green forests, uncivilized, with no written languages, no schools, no medicine. Most had never seen a doctor or a nurse. They were unaided and uncomforted in their pain. Their religion was the sacrifice of animals to appease the spirits and the offering of blood. The roads into their mountain trails had been badly cut up by the Viet Minh Communists during the last twelve years of war and had not yet been repaired.

Some of these tribes fortify their villages with sharp bamboo staves and place hidden bamboo spikes on the trails. These spikes are dipped in deadly poison mixed with decayed rat flesh. The people hide these lances under leaves on the pathway and if you should step on one, it would pierce through your shoe and bring death by poison and infection. On those jungle trails one might meet tigers, leopards, wild elephants, or snakes.

But *now* was the time to enter these great newly-accessible tribal areas. Unless we got to these tribes now, they would remain in their paganism. So we knew that we must lose no time in doing our part in bringing Christ to these "other sheep" — the Baru, Pakoh, Katu, Cua, Hrey, Bahnar, Bahnar-Cham, Sedang, Jeh and other tribes. Right now, with the long wars over, was the greatest challenge and greatest opportunity since 1941, for preaching the Gospel to these tribes and the Vietnamese in the hinterland. The vastness of eternity and the shortness of our lives, constrained us to move for God quickly.

To give our new venture a name for government recognition we organized our work under what we temporarily called, "Operation Service."

▶ 2 ◀
Survey

WE ARRIVED ON FEBRUARY 2ND in the blazing heat of noon. All of our little family, except Stanley, were in Viet Nam at this time — Leslie, Douglas and Ruth, and our grandchildren, Linda and Dougie.

Our son, Leslie, was doing well as a professional hunter, taking many American government personnel back into the jungles on elephant-back to hunt for big game. He had been having some terrific experiences with wild elephants, gaurs, wild buffaloes, tigers and bears.

A reporter told of one of his safaris: "The focus of the expedition was Leslie Smith, a 'Naturekind,' a 'Mowgli' — who was our professional guide. Les speaks the Raday tribal language and he swarms up the sides of immense elephants like a monkey. He tells game by the color of their eyes in the dark, and knows guns like Paderewski knew pianos."

Douglas and Ruth were in the American Embassy in Saigon. Douglas was in charge of the distribution of information films and mobile units through Viet Nam. We had never seen baby Dougie (now 1½ years old) and Gordon hadn't seen Linda, now four, since she was six days old. We'd been called "Grandfather" and "Grandmother" by our mountain people for years, as that is their title of honor, but now we really had a right to the names.

Da Nang was the logical place to start the survey of the tribes in Central Viet Nam. A seaport city, with a population of 120,000, it is in the middle of the central part of Viet Nam. For our missionary headquarters it was necessary to be in a city where proper banking and administrative facilities were available.

The Christian and Missionary Alliance had started work here fifty years before and have a fine church and Bible School in Da Nang — this latter is now moved to Nha Trang, 300 miles south. The purpose of our mission was to fill in the great gaps still existing among the untouched tribes and Vietnamese.

When we arrived at the airport of Da Nang, we rode in the Air-Viet Nam bus to the head office in town. Then Gordon and I each hired a *cyclo-pousse*, which is like a tricycle with a comfortable armchair in front. Our Vietnamese drivers wheeled us to the main hotel of the town with our suitcases propped up in front of us. As we bowled along through the streets, crowds of Vietnamese people peered at us, smiled and gaily greeted us along the way. The Vietnamese are a delightful people, so ready to be friends. They have thick black hair, calm, almond-shaped black eyes, fine ivory-yellow skin and high cheekbones. Men and women are small-boned, very slight, rarely more than 5 feet 2 inches tall. Passing the big market place, we saw hundreds of women in short white jackets, black trousers and immense mushroom-shaped bamboo hats, squatting by their baskets of white turnips, purple aubergines, brilliant red peppers, lettuce, sweet potatoes. We could smell the pungent Nuoc Mam sauce.

We began to use the first few Vietnamese words we were now starting to learn and called out to them as we passed, "*Chao Ong, Ba*" — "How do you do?"

For two weeks we lived in the main French Hotel as we waited for the house we were renting to be somewhat renovated and freshly whitewashed before we moved in. Some French officers had just vacated it.

The Hotel is on the main boulevard and the wide Da Nang river, flowing out to the sea, runs parallel to the street. Shade trees of great beauty grow all along the water's edge and there are vistas of mountains towering up on the sea shore — blue-green in the morning; like faint mist at noon; and a wall of purple at sunset. Fishing junks skim like butterflies down the river out to the sea and back again, their sails of yellow-matting filled out full in the breeze.

The beaches are superb and the swimming is excellent. The My Khe Beach runs along the sea for 15 or 20 miles, with a wide, uninterrupted stretch of soft beige sand, and the clear turquoise blue South China Sea foams in with a swishing sound.

From the Son Cha Beach we looked out upon the Da Nang Bay, where the sea laps against the great rocks along the shore. Mountain slopes rise up from this beach, a vivid green from base to summit, covered with jungle thickets and vines. Across the bay are the jagged walls of range after range of jungle mountains. We have seen the sun setting red there, incredibly beautiful, as the wine-rose rays illumine the waters in glorious shades and the sun descends behind the purple ranges.

The survey now began with intense studying of large maps and plans for many trips. We figured the area of the unreached tribes in Central Viet Nam would be larger than the Island of Formosa, some 400 miles in length from north to south. The maps showed us roads leading west from the main coastal highway, into what we knew must be tribal territory.

We also wanted to study the unreached tribes in Southern Laos and Northeast Cambodia, to tell the world of the need of the tribes in these countries.

Gordon's first long trip out from Da Nang in the Land Rover pick-up was across to Laos, taking our helper, Anh Hai, with him to cook and interpret. The two men drove 1200 miles to survey the tribes there. Three or four Swiss Plymouth Brethren had been solely responsible throughout the years for this whole southern area. These missionaries could not begin to handle it all, and they seemed willing to welcome a strong, evangelical mission to occupy the unreached areas. Gordon made a general survey to see where such a missionary society should establish main centers to reach the forty-five different tribes and dialects. Reports and photographs were sent back to America. Later we were glad that the Overseas Missionary Fellowship (C.I.M.) took on this big responsibility.

For the survey of Northeast Cambodia, we found a detailed map showing five tribes living in 192 villages in the unreached area of Stung Treng province. No missionary work had ever been done there.

Then began a seven months' intensive survey of the tribes of Central Viet Nam. To two of the tribes, the Christian and Mis-

Top: Ocean-going vessels come up the wide Da Nang River.
Left: A woven bamboo tub-boat used to paddle out to fishing junks.
Below: The superb My Khe beach of Da Nang.

sionary Alliance had sent two isolated Vietnamese workers for a number of years, but that was all. We could say that the whole area was practically unoccupied and we were the first missionaries ever to visit most of these tribes.

The survey meant long hikes up into the mountains, trips by sampan up rivers, and by Land Rover over terribly rough roads. We saw thrilling opportunities on all sides. We prayed to be given grace not to miss them.

Top: Son Cha Beach at Da Nang.
Below: Da Nang marketplace.

► 3 ◄
The Katu

WE FIRST VISITED the tribe nearest to Da Nang, the Katu people. With our Vietnamese cook, Anh Hai, Gordon and I drove ten miles to the Nam-O River and hired a big wooden sampan with five rowers to take us up the river far back into the jungles. For four hours we enjoyed the winding shallow river. Great jungle-clad mountains came down to the river's edge, blue and purple peaks towering behind and into the far distance. Brilliant birds were singing and there were butterflies as big as birds — black ones splashed with rose, or blue, or yellow.

Then the river narrowed and the big sampan couldn't go any farther. We stopped at a Vietnamese village on the river bank and hired a small sampan with two rowers. There were a number of Vietnamese villages in this area. "We've never heard this Good News," they said to us after we had explained a little of the Gospel to them. "When will you come back to tell us more?"

We rode up the river for two more hours, going through swift rapids and sometimes we had to get out and walk, while the two oarsmen pushed and pulled the boat over the stones and rapids.

The scenery was superb, the water was clear, and the mountains colorful. How we enjoyed the perfect weather.

Then we came to the end of navigation. The stream became too shallow. We left the sampan moored to the bank and climbed up to a wood-cutter's lean-to shack. It was too late then to go on to any tribe's villages up in the mountains, so we had a good swim in the river, an early supper and we put our camp-cots under a tarpaulin we had brought. With Anh Hai interpreting, we visited with the fifteen Vietnamese lumbermen at their shack and preached the Gospel to them. They, too, had never heard the message before. Then we went to bed early.

We were up next morning at 6 and had breakfast by 7 A.M., Anh Hai, Gordon and I, and a Vietnamese guide (one of the wood-cutters) started out on our trek to a Katu village. We knew that it was an unsubdued village, that the Katu in this section are still wild, semi-savage tribespeople, refusing ever to bow to any government, remaining independent, hidden in their mountains. The guide assured us that it was not far to the village, so we took no bedding or food with us — nothing except a canteen of water, a can of corned-beef and a can of fruit juice, thinking we could get some rice in the Katu village at noon and then we'd return to our cots and lean-to at night.

We walked two miles along a leafy trail by the rushing river. Then we crossed the rocky stream, wading through deep water, and began to climb a steep mountain. I thought we'd just be going up about a half-mile or so, so I enjoyed it even though it was steep and high. I've had a chronic heart-murmur ever since I was sixteen so I've seldom climbed mountains! But I stopped every few feet and counted ten and didn't get too much out of breath.

In some places we had to use our hands, grabbing at roots, to help us crawl up the steep trail. It was like going up a ladder.

After two more hours we must have reached 3000 feet. We thought the village must be near now, just a little way down the other side. I was still feeling pretty spry and it was exciting to have climbed so high. The guide was vague about the distance ahead.

We left the wood-cutters' trail now and we climbed along on a narrow "finger-nail" Katu trail at the edge of a mountain peak. Fortunately it was dry weather. We had barely a foothold and in wet weather it would be very slippery and dangerous.

At 2 P.M., when nearly worn out, we finally reached some tribe's rice fields — clearings on the steep, rocky mountain slopes, where they had burned down the forest and planted rice among stumps, fallen logs and stones. As we came out into the clearing from the wooded trail a great view of the surrounding mountain peaks like waves burst upon us — but I was getting too tired to enjoy it.

We followed the narrow trail down through the poor rice patches and sparse scrubby corn, until we saw some Katu men working. Our Vietnamese guide and Anh Hai, our "cook-inter-preter," went ahead of us to greet them and tell them who we were. Two well-muscled, stocky Katu men met us then, carrying the tallest iron-bladed spears we ever saw! Their brown bodies were naked except for loin-cloths. A band of cloth held their hair knobs. Gordon held out his hand to them, but they took no notice, saying in broken Vietnamese, "Don't know how salute."

They led the way another two miles to their village and this was truly hard and painful. We had climbed ten miles up and over the dreadful mountains! In all my life I've never walked more than two or three miles at the most in one stretch. Here I had *climbed* and descended over ten miles! How did I ever do it?

Nearing the village we passed a number of dangerous tiger traps — sharp bamboo spears held back by a bent sapling, ready to pierce the body when the trigger was stepped on. The Katu also put poisoned lances out on the trails hidden under leaves for the tigers, wild boars and other wild animals. We had to skirt these traps carefully. If one of these sharp spikes should pierce one's shoe and even just a little trace of the violent poison should enter his blood, he would be dead in a few moments. The poisoned arrow and lance kill the deer or wild pig but do not hurt the meat.

Then we went through a long arched tunnel to enter the village. The clearing was barricaded with fallen logs, thick brush and stones. There were seven little shacks in the village, built on the ground, walled with rough sheets of bark and thatched with palm-fronds. The people were wild and hid in their houses. These people, who had never seen white people before, peered out at us, afraid to come near. Some of the men wore black Vietnamese clothing and had their hair cut like the Vietnamese woodcutters, for they had traded with these woodcutters on the trail. The women wore short, coarsely-woven, navy-blue skirts and vests, with a band of bamboo around their hair. Some wore brass leggings to their knees and brass wire wound from their wrists to their elbows. Some of the men could understand a little Vietnamese, but the women didn't understand it at all.

One man placed a mat out for us on the ground in the center of the village and we fell down exhausted on it. Anh Hai tried to explain to them who we were — Americans, not French, against whom they have a great antipathy. The fact that we were un-armed and that I, a woman, was there, must have allayed some of their suspicion. Anh Hai told them that we had no food, so they brought us some boiled manioc root and tiny, hard corn cobs. We were glad to receive this even though it wasn't very appetizing. The people still hid in their huts peering out at us and muttering in their Katu language.

Gordon, thinking to make friends with them, as he had done many times among other tribes in the South, went over and took a picture on his Polaroid camera of one man squatting by his shack, and in a minute handed the man the picture. The Katu people were electrified! The man whose picture had been taken began to shout and yell, "Now I'll die! You've killed me! That evil eye in the middle of the black face has taken my shadow!" — The "shadow" to them means their soul. The sight of the perfect likeness of the man on the finished print meant that the soul had been extracted from the body and put on that paper. A soul-less tribesman may die immediately, or certainly he will fall ill. So the man was very frightened and began to dash all around the clear-ing. More of the people began to shout and were very angry.

In broken Vietnamese, the head man told Gordon that a sacri-fice would have to be made immediately in order to control the demons and get back the man's "soul." Gordon would have to pay thirty piastres (at that time about one dollar in value) as part of the sacrifice.

The sorcerer quickly set up an altar made of a tree stump, slashed a cut in a tree beside it and stuck the photo into the slash. Then he brought out a brass platter with some joss sticks, tobacco leaves and a bowl of alcohol, and placed it on the stump. Gordon had to lay his thirty piastres also down on the platter, and he did so, thinking there might have been trouble if he had refused. The sorcerer scattered rice around and made prodigious bounds and jumped up and down chanting rapidly to the demons for about fifteen minutes. All the villagers remained quietly back in their houses throughout the ceremony.

WAGGONER CHRISTIAN CHURCH

Top: Climbing the mountain to visit the Katu; Mrs. Smith and Anh Hai at left and young guide at right.

Left: The Katu whose picture Gordon had taken with the Polaroid arranges his "sacrifice." Picture is stuck on tree trunk at right.

Below: Sleeping mat in front of Katu house.

Gordon and I and our two Vietnamese men stood by, but all the time Gordon was secretly taking pictures of the Katu on his Rolleiflex camera which hung around his neck. This was unknown to the sorcerer as he danced and chanted. It's a good thing that the Katu didn't know what was going on!

The sorcerer now told Gordon to burn up the little photo before the altar as there was an evil spirit in it. The picture was still damp and wouldn't burn so the sorcerer made Gordon tear it all up into little bits and trample it into the ground.

After the sacrifice the sorcerer went with the others into their huts and we sat alone on the mat in the middle of the village. We knew that they were peeking at us from the cracks in their bark shacks. These people have no government authority over them. They pay no taxes. Their only touch with the outside world is as they trade in logs and rattan with the Vietnamese lumbermen.

They now began to lament that "because we were visiting them they would all die now." Our Vietnamese guide who knew a little of the Katu language could translate for us.

Now the tribesmen came out of their huts and planted tall spears, two before each of the seven huts! This was their sign of *hostility!* They didn't want us in the village and it looked dangerous for us.

We quickly told them that we came to them only as friends and that we had some presents of clothing for them. We brought out children's clothing, from our little grandchildren in Saigon, and some men's shirts and women's blouses from kind friends in America. They shouted and screamed that they wouldn't touch the clothes! — "If we took them we would all die!"

Gordon brought out eye medicine, malaria pills and sulfa pills for dysentery, but again they shouted that they wouldn't touch the medicine. "We'd all die if we took it." Their high-pitched angry voices sounded like hens cackling.

We patiently told them, through Anh Hai and the guide as interpreters, that we would have to spend the night in the village as it was too late and too dangerous to return down the trail now. There were the poison lances on the trail at night and also the terrible arrows set in the hidden traps for deer and tigers. We dare not go over the narrow trails in the dark. We couldn't have seen a foot ahead of us. Tigers and others wild beasts were now roaming in the deep forests.

But we also wondered if it were safe for us to stay in the village! Our having the guide and Anh Hai along helped greatly. If we had been alone, just two white strangers, they would never have let us into the village, or if we had come in, they, themselves, would have all run away, or they would have killed us. They told all of this to our guide and cook. The Viet Minh Communist propaganda to them in the past years (during the war with the French) had been, "Defend yourselves against strangers — the white man. They come to take your riches! They insult you." But Anh Hai assured them over and over that we were only there to be their friends.

The cook interceded with the Katu to give us a hut for the night. He tried to impress on them how cold we'd be, sleeping out on the mat in the center of the village all night. We were 3000 feet above sea level and it gets very cold at that height at night. And we had no blankets. It might even rain! The cook threatened them a bit (he told us) and so, finally, one man said we could move into his hut. Before he let us move in, however, this Katu took out a lot of his own things from the hut and made a sacrifice over the board bed to the spirits, to appease them because they would be angry at our presence. The two long spears were planted outside the door.

We were happy to move into the tiny shack and have some shelter for the night. The owner had a nice hand-woven bamboo hammock and I swung in that and rested. Gordon sprayed some D.D.T. over the board bed and around the hut and the owner again became suspicious and scared, but we told him that this would kill the dangerous malaria mosquitoes (we had no nets), fleas and other bugs. Anh Hai built up a warm wood fire on the mud floor inside the hut for us and he and the guide also had a wooden bed for themselves in the shack.

Before dark, I took out a flannelgraph story to show to the people. The background was of red flannel and as I started to hang it up in the center of the village, the people shouted, "Take that away!" One man came running at me, gesturing fiercely. Then we surmised that the people had probably had trouble because of the Communist Red flag! Perhaps they had not obeyed the Viet Minh Communists and someone had been killed or maybe Vietnamese Democratic Nationalist soldiers had come and punished their village for following the Communist Reds. They would not explain, but they were determined not to have my red flannelgraph background up in the village, so I had to put it quickly away.

But I was still eager to show them the pictures. I held up a picture of Christ on the cross and tried to tell them of His great love for them, so great that He had died as a Sacrifice for their sins to save them eternally in a wonderful place called heaven. They were terrified of the pictures and they all ran into their huts again and banged their doors shut.

Gordon tried to be friendly, squatting before each hut and trying to say a few nice words to them but they wouldn't listen to him or invite him into their huts.

I entered the door of a shack but they told me to leave as there was sickness there. I saw a poor woman on a board bed covered from head to foot in a bamboo mat. We offered good pills for malaria to her — Camoquin — but again the people refused it. They cried, "She's sick because she has no pig for a sacrifice to the demons. Give us a pig to sacrifice for her and she'll get well." I tried again to tell about the Sacrifice the Chief of the Skies had made for her by giving the Prince of Heaven, His own Son — but they refused to listen.

When it was dark we went into our little hut, closed the bark door, built up the fire and tried to sleep without blankets or pillows on the hard boards. We put on some of the American clothes we had brought to give to the people, to try to keep warm.

At 6 o'clock, sharp at dawn, we were ready to leave the village. We offered the people clothes and medicines again and even left some of the nice little children's clothes in the hut for them, but they ran after us with them, saying, "We couldn't take anything or the spirits would make us die."

Most of the way back down the mountain was a slipping and sliding adventure. It meant bracing and much strain on the legs to keep from stumbling and pitching headlong down the 75° inclines. Again I say I couldn't have done it if Gordon hadn't been ahead of me holding one of my hands braced against his shoulder, supporting a lot of my weight and showing me where to step down next. Sometimes we had to just skid down the dew-slippery trail in the dense forest. Fortunately I had on a good strong pair of flat shoes — American Keds — and Gordon had on his canvas shoes with thick rubber treads. My feet didn't hurt or blister at all and the shoes clung to the sheer rocks and rubble of the trail.

Then at noon (and we could hardly believe it), we were actually down at the bottom and there was the glorious river! We'd been climbing down steadily for six hours. I hobbled right into the cool, clear, deep river with all my clothes and shoes on. It revived me. I just lay in it and put my face down into it. Oh, the cool, healing water to wash away the sweat and blood from the blood-suckers and to counteract the aching pains!

Soon our guide and the boatmen arrived from our camp with our Nestle's powdered coffee. Some lumbermen by the river had a fire and bucket and we boiled water for the coffee. How it revived us! My painful muscles seemed to be easing up. We waded through the river and walked back the last two miles to the camp.

Where was our faithful Anh Hai? He had followed the boat-men and guide with our food, but he got behind them and took a wrong trail. He was gone for two hours. He had walked up another mountain and came in sight of more Katu rice fields. These were the villages we had seen on the map and to which we thought our guide was taking us! They were much closer and easier to access. Anh Hai came upon a fine troop of gibbon apes, beige and black, on the trail and they "wah-wahed" at him and scared him badly.

How we enjoyed the sampan trip down the river again. I lay, exhausted, on our blankets, in the bottom of the boat and didn't get out for the rapids and shallow parts. They just dragged me and the boat through them. We glided down for eight hours and the moon shone down full upon us. The river was glassy and peaceful and we dozed to the sound of the paddles dipping. What relief and rest after that hard mountain trail!

Reaching Nam-O near midnight, we got into our Land Rover again and within an hour we were home in bed in Da Nang.

► 4 ◄
Digging In

Now that we were moved up to Central Viet Nam with our headquarters in Da Nang, we must learn the Vietnamese language which is, of course, the main language of the country.

A pleasant young Christian Vietnamese girl came to us soon after we arrived in Da Nang and offered to be our language teacher. Her name was Thanh Hoa, meaning "Blue Flower."

Each district in Viet Nam has its own dialect of the language. The city of Hue, sixty miles north of Da Nang, has a dialect of different accents. Even out in the country, just a few miles away from the city of Da Nang, the people pronounce some of the words differently. But we missionaries are taught to speak the pure Central Viet Nam dialect of the city of Da Nang.

We found the sing-song language very musical. When well-spoken in a pleasant voice it is truly a delight to hear.

How we would be able to serve God among these people when we could understand their language and they could understand us! Language proficiency would quicken our appreciation of their thoughts, beliefs, needs and reactions. Equipped with facility in this tongue, we could help train valuable national workers to aid in the evangelization of this land.

Vietnamese is the trading language of this country with its white people, Chinese, Indians, and with the tribespeople. We could use Vietnamese to begin our work among the tribes, rather than delaying their evangelization for more years by waiting until each tribal language had been mastered. Of course, in the main, only the men of the tribes' villages nearest the Vietnamese outposts could speak Vietnamese. Most of the women of the tribes

Top left: Buddhist priests gather for meeting at Da Nang.

Top right: Ornate screen of Buddhist mythical figures in front of Buddhist Temple in Da Nang; and interior of one of the Buddhist temples in Da Nang.

Below: One of the Buddhist temples of Da Nang.

Top: A group of Vietnamese high school girls.
Below: Vietnamese girls of Da Nang.

and the tribesmen farther in the interior, did not know it at all. But we could preach to them through a tribal interpreter who knew Vietnamese well and could interpret the message to his people. So we had the priceless advantage of immediate entry into the tribal villages, using Vietnamese.

The Christian and Missionary Alliance have made a splendid translation of the Bible into Vietnamese and also have translated an excellent hymn book of over 450 hymns. They also have many Christian books and tracts translated. So we could begin to study the Scriptures immediately in the Vietnamese language.

Hour after hour, day after day, we had to practice our vocabularies. I began to learn some simple Bible stories by heart and invited the neighbor children in every Sunday afternoon for a children's meeting out under the big, shady trees that spread a canopy in our backyard. Thanh Hoa and some of her friends would come to help me in these meetings. Soon the children were lustily singing gospel hymns and enjoying flannelgraph stories.

Many Vietnamese young people began to come to our house, pleading with me to give them English lessons for an hour or two each day. I began to take them on and soon had a class of twenty young men and women every evening eagerly studying out on our veranda. It was a chance to get acquainted with these Vietnamese people.

We found them fascinating. Their long, slanting eyes, set shallow in their faces, are as black as onyx under water and the whites are clear. Their skins are cream-pale and their lips are full. Their hands and feet are narrow with slender, tapering fingers.

The girls wear sheath-like tunics down to the toes — with a long panel back and front, meeting tightly at the tiny waist and under the arms. The tunic falls loosely from this tight-fitted bodice over long white satin trousers. The waist fits so snugly you would think the girl had been sewn into it. It is a costume for the slim, lissome, graceful, erect figures of the Vietnamese women. Often it is made of filmy silk or nylon in lovely blossom colors. The tunic is their street and visiting costume. For work they remove it and just have the simple white jacket that is worn underneath and the trousers. The women love to wear good jewelry — a delicate gold necklace, dainty earrings, bracelets and rings.

The men now all favor European dress.

They are a refined, delicate people in many ways — with gentle, soft-speaking voices. They have an avid desire for education and are eager to learn English. Their capacity for memorizing is outstanding. English is now the foreign language of choice.

Vietnamese fishermen drawing in their net in the bay of Da Nang.

► 5 ◄

Meet Chesty and Hopalong

WHEN WE RETURNED FROM our trip to the Katus we found that our two gibbon apes, "Chesty, the Bushman" and "Hopalong," whom we had had for over three years in Banmethuot, were coming back to us.

When we went home on furlough in 1955, we sold our apes to a young American pilot and he had flown them over with him in his plane to Thailand. Now we were anxious to buy them back again, so he was flying them back to us, free of charge, on one of his frequent trips to Da Nang. They arrived here in the pilot's plane all the way from Bangkok, riding comfortably in a nice big basket full of cool green leaves.

We had a rustic cage-house made for them and they were soon happily swinging around by their long arms on the bars, shelves and rings in the cage.

They were beautiful pets — the best pets we've ever owned. They were both fully grown now and were three feet high. Gibbons have black satin, wistful, brooding faces, very human-looking, with finely hooked, delicate noses, thin-lipped straight mouths, firmly set, that quiver upon the slightest emotion. They have big, melancholy dark eyes with no whites — the whole eye is brimful of deep brown. These animals have a crest of soft, black fur on the top of their heads and creamy-white side-whiskers. Their black fur is thick, clean and shining. Gibbons have extremely slender, long, furry arms with long, kid-gloved black hands and fingernails. Their arms are those of great climbers for they clamber up swiftly and swing along among the treetops. On the other hand, their legs are short like little stubs, as they are not ground animals but live in the highest jungle trees.

Gibbons are the finest acrobats in the world — swinging easily, lightly among the branches, graceful and deft. Holding both arms in the air for balance, they can run on their short legs along a branch and then launch again on their dives through the foliage. One can watch them fascinated for hours. What beauty of movement, full of grace and power, as they "brachiate" in the trees, swinging arm over arm like boys down the "traveling rings" of a gymnasium.

And their strange, whooping calls, in loud, clear voices! They are called the "prima donnas of the jungle." They greet the rising sun, opening their mouths wide and singing with all their hearts in long, drawn-out calls — marvelous and thrilling to hear. They start at the bottom of the scale and go whooping, whooping, whooping up and up until they reach a very high note, then they trill down the scale again, their voices echoing far and wide.

When they rest, they lie flat on their backs with perhaps one leg cocked over the other and one arm tucked under the head.

Very affectionate by nature, the apes who live with people come to show an intense craving for human affection and companionship and are quite happy in captivity if they receive these. Not to have given Chesty and Hopalong affection would have been as brutal as to have beaten them.

They have good memories and so knew us when they returned to us again, even after a year. As we would near their cage, they would make small noises of delight and as we entered the cage with them, they would fling themselves in our arms, their long arms wound tightly around our necks, and sing their hearts out.

Our house-girl, Chi Nga, was very kind and faithful in helping to care for them.

In a non-Christian country like Viet Nam it is an important lesson to the people to have animals that are loved and cared for. We are often shocked by the cruelty of the orientals toward animals. They do not treat their dogs and cats as we treat ours in the West. They have them mainly as "livestock" to be eaten whenever they feel like it. So they are not petted and fondled and made much of. The people are quite indifferent to the suffering of animals. The cause of this lies in their Buddhist doctrine. They think that if a person is evil in this life he will become an animal

Left: The author and Hop-a-long, great friends.
Below: Hop-a-long, the Gibbon ape. When young, he had soft beige fur which later turned black.

in his next incarnation. Therefore, they think that every animal may have been once a wicked human being and they feel contempt for them.

Chesty, the black-coated skalawag, would sometimes get out of the cage and chase the Vietnamese girls, legging it after them down the street on his tiny stubs of legs and waving his long arms in the air to balance himself like a drunken sailor, while they all scattered, screaming, away.

Chesty swinging in the trees behind the Smith home.

▶ 6 ◀
The Cua

THE GOOD FELLOWSHIP through the letters and fervent, intercessory prayers of our friends in America made us feel actually lifted along, as if great spiritual forces were in motion to help in this work. How grateful we were and full of praise to our Heavenly Father.

Gordon had a big map of Central Viet Nam up on his study wall and he soon had thirty pins into places on it that must be opened up now, as new strategic centers among the different wild tribes. It was exciting to begin exploring this land.

One of our first trips would be into a place called Tra Bong, a center for the Cua tribe. On the map we could see a side road off from the main coastal highway, leading into the mountains, about thirty miles west of the town of Quang Ngai, which is one hundred miles south of Da Nang.

Along the coastal road there is a great deal of traffic — bicycles, Vespa-scooters, motorcycles, and big military cars. There are many native buses packed with passengers, with several hanging on the back and piled high with cargo on top. They sway dangerously and sometimes go over the banks.

Many men and women jog along on foot, bent under shoulder-poles which support fifty pounds of weight in grain or other produce, at either end.

Out in the fields are the little thatched mud and bamboo huts of the farmers, surrounded by clusters of bamboo, bananas, and coconut palms.

We passed through many scores of villages and towns and had long, tedious waits getting across ferries, where the fine French bridges had been blown out during the wars.

36

When we finally reached Quang Ngai, we went first to see the Vietnamese Provincial Administrator. It was a blistering hot day of 90° but his shady office was cool with electric fans and he had iced soft drinks for us. We studied a huge map of his province. He pointed out strategic places that we could visit. What hands on a man! — long, pale and delicately shaped, with a great Jade ring on one tapered finger. Hundreds of generations of high civilization had made those truly aristocratic hands.

The places in this District were Tra My, Bong Mieu, Tra Bong, Son Ha, Gi Liang, Bato and Gia Vuc — all important and populous market places for the tribes, and until now, they had never been touched by a missionary.

After the visit, we started out immediately for Tra Bong, two and one-half hours away over bad roads into the interior. The stone roads had been so cut up during the war that they were only makeshift trails now. They had never been macadamized and were full of potholes and the trenches dug by the Communists.

There was plenty of dust and the handkerchief I had brought along that morning was now quite brown and our clothes were very dusty. But bad as the roads were, we were glad that they were there and that we could travel over them. Our strongly built Land Rover could go over anything.

The mountains were looming straight ahead of us now, intensely blue and purple. One high peak had sharp saw-teeth and was the landmark for Tra Bong. We passed through miles of rice fields and sugar cane again. Viet Nam is a nation of farmers. They are the backbone of the country. There were dozens of little villages and hamlets with their market places, all absolutely unreached by the Gospel. All along the people seemed friendly and open-hearted. The Viet Minh Communist war had been strong here and every French home and good building had been completely bombed out. All the houses now were just miserable shacks of mud and bamboo.

For many miles in the area, the steel rails and ties of the railroad tracks of the main line going to Saigon, had been pulled up and the people made their bridges out of them. These rails of steel were a tremendous temptation for a native blacksmith.

As we neared Tra Bong, steep rocky hills came down to the

Top: The Land Rover can go through almost anything.
Below: At the Tra Bong market with the Cua tribespeople (cinnamon bark in the bundles at their feet).

Left: A Cua tribesgirl.
Right: Gathering cinnamon bark.

Below: Preparing to load up with cinnamon bark and go to market in Da Nang.

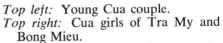

Top left: Young Cua couple.

Top right: Cua girls of Tra My and Bong Mieu.

Left: Cua tribesmen, their mouths stained with red betel-nut juice.

Below right: A wild Cua tribesman. He believes he would die if he ever washed his hair.

Below left: Cua tribesgirls in their native finery. The man is a Christian soldier.

road. There were big rock masses and the stony soil looked too poor for crops.

Then we reached Trail's End — the Vietnamese village of Tra Bong. This was the last settlement of the yellow men, before going into the brown-skinned tribespeople of the mountains. The little thatched mud Vietnamese shacks were strung out all along the last part of this road for two miles or so, making the main street of the village. This was the trading post for the Cua tribe of 20,000 people. Their great mountains of jungle wilderness spread like a horseshoe around the little village.

We went to the head village official's house and he was very friendly. One of the members of his office staff said we could stay in his house — the only brick house left standing in the village. It was old, crude and black with mildew, but cool and with lots of room for us. The owner had planted fruit trees thickly in the yard and through our open window we could look out at coconut palms, pomolos, cinnamon-apple trees, papayas, jack-fruit trees and slender areca-nut palms. Besides the fragrance of blossoms from these trees, we also inhaled the lovely smell of cinnamon-stick candy! We found that one half of the veranda was piled high with rolls of cinnamon bark, cut, dried and arranged neatly to sell in Da Nang, and from there to be shipped to America or some other market in the world. We learned that it was the Cua tribespeople who brought down this cinnamon bark, in huge loads on their backs, from their trees up in the mountains and sold it at the Tra Bong market.

As we put up our camp — cots and nets — visitors came flocking into our house to see us. A white man hadn't been seen here for fifteen years and many of them had never seen a white woman before. We said we'd like to have a meeting in the village that night and the Vietnamese official said we could have one in the market place which was one-half mile away.

We were glad to have Anh Hai prepare an evening meal for us and we tried to get a little rest, for we were nearly cripples after the jolting trip.

Then by our gas-pressure light, we went to the market and set up our flannelgraph board and at least 100 people came crowding around for the evening meeting. Gordon and I took turns in telling the Creation Story, the Crucifixion and the Rich Man and Lazarus from the graphic pictures, with Anh Hai translating from French into Vietnamese. The whole crowd accompanied us back to the house and we felt a bit like Christ must have felt when whole villages of people walked down the road with Him.

It was very hot and we slept with all the doors and windows open to the bright moonlight. Two Vietnamese guards were in the room with us with loaded guns to protect us against any Viet Minh Communists who might be sneaking around, for even though the wars were over at that time and the Geneva Treaty signed, still there were some Communists hiding back in the mountains ready to do harm.

Early next morning we were at the Tra Bong market to see the crowds of Cua tribespeople coming down from the mountains to trade. What a picturesque sight they were! Immediately we named them "The Blue Bead People" as they wear masses of sky blue beads strung on circles of stiff wire around their necks — piled up in tier upon tier — until it looked as if their heads were sticking up through blue life-belts. Some also wear bands of beads around their ankles and encircling their hair. Many of the girls wore marvelous wide belts made of hundreds of strings of tiny, many-colored beads around their hips — wide at the back and the strings all brought together tapering in a tie in front. They wear this belt over a short, dark cotton skirt.

The men had their ears pierced and wore long spike earrings, pointing forward and backward, made out of pewter and fine black wire. Some of these long stems curled through the ears and ended in tight little rolls. They were all handmade by the tribesmen — very artistic and really flashy!

We had never seen tribal ornaments like these before. The blue beads set off their brown bodies handsomely. The men mostly wore just a loin-cloth. The women wore the short, dark skirt and a halter-like blouse. They have lively, black, deep-set eyes looking out from under black, heavy, tangled, curly hair. Some had their hair cut in bangs, straight across from ear to ear and hanging to their shoulders in the back, or rolled up into a big knob held with a homemade comb of wood with pewter trimmings.

Nearly all of them carried huge bundles of green tea leaves or cinnamon bark on their backs to sell to the Vietnamese. What terribly heavy loads these were and many of the Cuas were just poor little children staggering under the awful weight. I tried to lift a bundle but couldn't move it. Great bartering went on in the market place, with the Vietnamese eagerly buying up the tea and valuable cinnamon bark at low prices. Since that time, the price for cinnamon has been regulated by the government so that there won't be so much cheating of the Cua tribespeople.

These Cuas who come down to the market understand quite a bit of Vietnamese. Their own Cua language has never been written down. What a task for white missionaries!

We handed out some medicines to the poor people — especially pills for malaria fever — to begin to make friends with them.

The head Chief of the Cua tribe for this Tra Bong section met us at the market and asked us to come to visit his village up a mountain-side nearby. We climbed the quarter-mile up and there were eight Cua houses — just a small village of about seventy people. Most of these Cuas living so close to Tra Bong were dressed in just ordinary Vietnamese clothing.

We visited the Cua houses. Some were about seventy feet long, built on stilts far above the ground. We went up a shaky notched pole ladder to the house. All the rooms are along one side of the Cua house and are joined by a long side veranda. The rooms are small, dark, smoky, with fires in open mud fire-boxes. There were alcohol jars against the walls; spears and cross-bows in the thatched roof; and dried meat hanging in the smoke over the fires, some of it quite evil-smelling.

Although the Cua chief is fairly rich for a tribesman, he said that he, or any of the others, couldn't build any new houses now because the Communists, hiding back in the mountains, would come and burn down any nice, new longhouse. So all of their houses were old, black and rickety. Pigs and chickens dug in the muck underneath the houses. But the verandas are pleasant and have splendid views over the deep valley down below, with a river running through it and the mountains towering up beyond.

The Cua tribespeople fish in the rivers, hunt with traps and arrows, raise small crops on the stony mountain sides, and sell their cinnamon bark and tea.

We met the chief's fine son, Long — a straight, handsome young man, who walked deliberately and was assured of the respect of his village as the son of this very influential chief. His wife, Huong (meaning "Rose"), was an attractive young woman. We were agreeably surprised to find that both Long and Huong could read and write Vietnamese well. It was the Viet Minh Communists who had taught them and some others of the bright young people in Tra Bong when they occupied this village during the war years. They had held night classes for the village, forcing the young people to study.

The chief and his wife gave us refreshing green coconut milk to drink. Then he had the people play their gongs and tom-toms to welcome us to their village. The Cuas play the gongs differently from other tribes that we know. They have a remarkably deep, soft musical effect as they beat on the big bronze discs with one hand muffled in wads of cloth, and then stop the sound now and then with the elbow, to make a syncopated beat.

We were able to preach briefly to the people that morning but the chief wanted us to return that night for a special meeting he would arrange for all the village.

We'll never forget our meeting that night in this mountain-side Cua village — our first with just the Cua people. We showed flannelgraphs for an hour or so and the tribal audience was spell-bound. To our great joy the Chief's son, Long, and his wife, Huong, came forward to commit their lives to the Saviour that night. Another bright young tribesman was there from his village across the river. His name was Quang and he invited us to visit his people the next day, arranging to meet us and take us there.

So the next afternoon we went over with Quang. Long and Huong also came with us. We walked along a path through rice fields — mostly winding in and out on top of the narrow dikes which separate the muddy rice plots.

Quang's village was a huddled group of dejected black bamboo houses raised up on poles, as a protection against wild animals. The village was right at the foot of a great mountain. Inside, the houses were encrusted with smoke, soot, cobwebs and dirt. Spears and cross-bows were on the walls. The people here, too, lived in these dreadful old huts, so that the Communists wouldn't be tempted to burn down their village.

One of Quang's brothers is a big chief for this area on this side of the river and he and all the families of Quang's relatives — who made up the village — welcomed us kindly. The chief had some of the young people do a tribal dance to welcome us. Three pretty young Cua girls swayed and circled with upheld arms to the rhythm of the gongs and the booming of a large drum beat upon by several men, also marching around in the circle.

Then the chief called for silence and told the people to listen to us as we gave our message. We sang a hymn or two for them in Vietnamese. Then we set up our flannelgraph board and showed the story of Creation, Anh Hai translating into Vietnamese and Quang translating into Cua.

This was a memorable hour indeed. Never before had the Cua chief and his people heard the Gospel. They had never heard the name of God before. After the story of Creation and man's sin, we told of the coming of Christ to this sinful world as our Redeemer. We showed flannelgraphs on the crucifixion, resurrection and ascension, in beautiful portrayals.

It was all like a glimpse of wonderland to the people. To hear of this great eternal salvation, through the sacrifice of God's Son on the cross, was a tremendous enlightenment for them. Quang, and his brother, the chief, and Ut, his sister (one of the pretty girls) and in fact, practically the whole group asked how they could become Christians.

What joy to see them believe so quickly! It seemed as if they had just been waiting for us to come and they accepted the message easily and simply. God had their hearts prepared. The seed had fallen on good ground. "The gospel is the power of God unto salvation to everyone that believeth."

The mountains were masses of purple now against an orange-pink sky and we had to hasten back to our camping house as a tiger or leopard might be coming down from the mountains to prowl for dogs, pigs, cattle or human beings who weren't safely under shelter.

Next morning as we were packing up to go on to another new tribe — the Hreys, who are neighbors to the Cuas — the five young new believers, Long, Huong, Quang, his wife and Ut all came to go with us. They would accompany us on this trip to the Hreys, and give their testimony of their new-found faith in Christ. Then they would return with us to Da Nang to study the Word of God. After some months they would go back to preach the truths they had learned to their own people.

Mr. Long, at the right, was the first Cua tribesman to believe in Christ. His wife, Rose, is in the center. Mr. Hap, at the left, was the Vietnamese evangelist at Tra Bong for several years and helped build up the active church there.

WAGGONER CHRISTIAN CHURCH

▶ 7 ◀

The Hrey

From Tra Bong we drove back to the main highway near Quang Ngai and then went down another side road for 30 miles leading into the mountains to Son Ha, an important center for the Hrey tribespeople.

Again we went crashing over deep cuts in the worn-out stone roads. Our Land Rover was a regular "Covered Wagon" bumping and jolting us along as we pioneered. It was amazing how the car stood all the pits, ruts and holes.

After a couple of hours or so we came to the Son Ha River valley. We stopped the car in speechless admiration of the view — a breath-taking vista of valley, river and surrounding mountains. The Son Ha River was foaming on the rocks. The air was alive with the voice of the rushing water.

Who are these Hrey tribespeople? They number 90,000 souls — the largest tribe in Central Viet Nam. They live back of Quang Ngai in these Hrey River valleys of Son Ha, Gi Liang and Bato and reach up into the massive mountains between Gia Vuc and toward Kontum. Some of these mountains are 5,400 feet high. For seven months of the year they are cold with flooding rains. But the Hrey tribespeople are proud of their warm fertile valleys, where they cultivate wet rice fields and also grow some corn, tobacco, sweet potatoes and cotton.

Many Viet Minh Communists were in this area during the years of war with the French. Terrible battles were fought in these valleys with great massacres on both sides. The Hrey helped the French against the Viet Minh. At one time the Hrey killed 5000 Viet Minh, throwing their bodies into the river or burning

47

them. Then the Viet Minh returned for reprisals, killing and setting fires in their turn.

As we drove along toward the village of Son Ha we passed terraced rice fields on the mountain slopes and river banks, like slabs of cool, green jade.

Each family carefully tends their small amount of land. Scores of Hrey villages with longhouses up on posts are almost hidden in among groves of graceful, tall, slender areca-nut palms. These are the nuts used with the betel vine-leaf for chewing. The Hrey tribespeople chew this nut and leaf profusely, even more so than the Vietnamese.

Anh Hai and the Cua young people we had with us, all made themselves comfortable on the benches of the government pavilion lent to us for camping, spreading out their own bamboo mats.

After lunch and rest, we all had a refreshing swim in the swift flowing Son Ha River. Then we went out to visit a Hrey village. What scores and scores of villages were within our reach! By our map we could see that there are hundreds of tribal villages down this Son Ha River for twenty miles or more. There are also thousands of Vietnamese people lining the roads from the main highway into Son Ha who had never yet heard the Gospel. We asked God for a good Vietnamese evangelist to put into this place immediately to reach some of these multitudes.

As we entered one Hrey village, we saw some svelte young women coming up the pathway from the river, carrying jars of water on their heads. The Hrey women wear long black cotton skirts, each with a peplum. Older women coming into the village were loaded down with their baskets of wood for their fires. The liana shoulderstraps of the baskets sawed into their shoulders. All were chewing the betel nut and spitting jets of crimson saliva. There were mothers going about their various duties with babies strapped to their backs, with only their little bare feet visible in front. Troops of water buffaloes, brought in by little naked boys, came slowly back to their enclosures in the village for the night. Under the long bamboo houses up on stilts were black, sway-back pigs grunting in the mud. Fowl were clucking and quacking among the houses.

Up on a fine veranda at the front of his longhouse was the chief

Top: Terraced rice fields like slabs of cool, green jade; Hrey longhouses.
Center: The author playing ukelele and singing gospel songs.
Below: A Hrey longhouse with bamboo walls and thatched roof.

Top: Hrey chief in black coat and pants welcomed author to his longhouse. Note notched tree-trunk "stairs" into house.
Below: Evangelistic party visiting a Hrey village.

Top left: Sacrificial pole in Cua village; it is trimmed with dabs of white cotton.

Right: Water buffalo being sacrificed at Phu Hoa, Katu village.
Below: Animal is tormented, cut with knives and pierced with spears. People believe that through his death their village will be protected from evil spirits.

Top right: Cua tribesman beats his tom-tom, marching around sacrifice.

Top left: Hrey sorcerer offers a chicken sacrifice to appease demons who have brought sickness to baby in house behind him.

Left: Men and women march around sacrifice in center of circle.

Below: Hrey woman with baby; Hrey man, now a believer, cuts off strings signifying his pact with the devil.

of the village. He was wrinkled and skinny, naked except for his loin-cloth. He had necklaces of black and white beads around his neck (when he dies, he will pass these treasures on to his son). The standard beads of the Hrey people are black and white. We saw no blue Cua beads here. When the old chief grinned at us he showed the stumps of his teeth, red with betel-nut juice.

This great Hrey tribe follows the practice of cutting out their six top front teeth when they are children, just as the Raday, Mnong, Stieng, Jarai and other tribes do in the south. Of all the scores of tribes in Viet Nam, the Katu and the Cua are the only two that do not follow this hideous practice.

The chief welcomed us up to see his longhouse. It was a good building made of braided bamboo walls and heavily thatched roof, all built up on seven-foot posts.

We climbed the tall notched tree-trunk to the veranda. The floor was made of split bamboo with a railing around it. We bent over to go into the narrow door-frame of the house which was ornamented with chicken feet, fish tails and feathers to keep out evil spirits. We also entered into a cloud of wood smoke from the open fires which filled the room and stung the eyes. This long room of about two hundred feet was the sleeping and living room of five or six families, all related. Each family had their own clay fire-box, cooking pots and mats. Only the fire separates each household. On the walls were swords, cross-bows, spears and shields made of the hides of buffaloes.

Women pounded the rice, three of them at a time, at one mortar made from a tree trunk. This was fastened into the floor in the center of the longhouse on a support reaching down to a firm base in the ground below. Lifting and lowering in rhythm, the women beat their heavy pestles of wood on the rice, hulling and grinding it. They pounded hard, jerking the whole of their supple bodies, their black hair flowing down as they worked. This was extremely hard labor.

The Cua young people could not understand the Hrey language. A high mountain range separates these two tribes. As was the case with the Cua, the Hrey language had never been put into writing.

We heard some weird chanting nearby so went to see what

was happening. A fragile altar of split bamboo had been set up beside one of the longhouses. It was surmounted by frizzed-out pompoms of bamboo and on some banana leaves were offerings of rice and bits of a chicken for the spirits. A sorcerer, a young man, was trying to appease the demons who had brought sickness upon a little child in the longhouse. He had killed a chicken and was now calling on the spirits. Every now and then he would leap high in the air before his small bamboo altar and let out a cry that would freeze one in terror.

We showed some flannelgraphs telling the people that no demons can be where Jesus Christ is worshiped. He will deliver them and He bids them, "Come unto Me and I will give you rest." A large crowd gathered to hear and showed interest.

That night there was a big sacrifice of a water buffalo in another nearby village. Sacrifices are so dear to the heart of these wild tribespeople! This religion of primitive animism is deeply entrenched in their souls. How they love to set up the great sacrificial pole with its high cross-arms all painted in red and black weird designs! Decorating the poles are the great pompoms of curled, frizzed and flossed bamboo, shaped into cones, trumpets and pennants, floating in the breeze of evening. The water buffalo to be sacrificed is tied with a heavy braided rattan rope to this pole. The buffalo is the most noble beast of the tribespeople, and in the sacrifice he incarnates the devil. He represents the evil spirit which dries up the rice harvest, kills people and herds of buffaloes and cows by sickness. Tonight all these evils would fall on the buffalo victim. He would be offered up at dawn.

Now comes the march of men and women around the pole and the animal. The men hold big gongs on cords and several tom-toms, beating them as they march, with mallets enveloped by cloth. The sound is at first smothered, then suddenly vibrates and becomes rapid and sonorous. They pull out of the gongs sounds that are deep and harmonious. The beat goes up to a violent crescendo — then becomes veiled and dies down to a sound like a breeze softly blowing — then it vibrates up again. Accompanying the gongs is the low throbbing beat of the big tom-toms.

This music is the joy of living for these tribespeople. They pull voices out of these bronze discs. They make the bronze sing!

The several young women marching in the ring, clap their hands and lift their arms to the sky. Their clapping in these sacrifices does not mean joy, but means that they are railing at the devil and reviling him.

At intervals, the leading men cry out in unearthly, shrill cries to frighten away the demons.

The moon shines on the scene and the orange light of resin torches flickers here and there.

Jars of rice alcohol, each containing about twenty quarts, are uncovered now. A man pulls out the leaves which serve as the cork in the neck. Supple bamboo stems are placed in each brown, glossy jar, and the jars now look like monstrous spiders with all the tubes, like legs, sticking out. The tribespeople gather around to drink through the night.

Then the sorcerer, like an apparition, his mouth blackened by betel-nut chewing, his hair long, dirty and gray, his eyes deep-set and hard, comes to chant the formula to the spirits. He wears only a loin-cloth, with beads and bone necklaces around his neck. He has bracelets of brass on his bony arms and legs.

He ties cords of cotton on the wrists of those who have given the buffalo for the sacrifice. These cords will cause the evil spirits to flee away. He prays for the spirits of the mountains, water, wind and fire to guard them and give them good health and happiness.

Again the gongs and tom-toms ring out as the dance continues around the buffalo. Now and then someone goes to the poor animal, curses him, hits him and then goes back to drink some more. The innocent beast turns about the pole, tearing at the strong lianas. He paws the ground and cries out pitifully.

As dawn comes, the men gather with their long spears around the poor buffalo, made crazy by fatigue and the pain from the jabs he has received through the night. The gongs and drums beat. As the sun rises, the animal is cut and pierced with swords and spears. The blood flows. How inhuman and cruel it is! Blows on the gongs! Strikes of the spears! The moaning of the poor animal! As the sun rises, the buffalo kneels, defeated and is still. The main thrust of the spear is full in his heart. The poor buffalo tries to get up — pounds his hoofs, falls, facing the sun. Now the village will be under the protection of the sun god!

The sorcerer takes the blood and traces designs on the house to protect from evil spirits.

The people cut up the meat and roast it on open fires for a feast. The head of the buffalo will ornament the top of the first pole. It will dry out up there — offered to the sun. The dogs grab the bones. The pigs eat the intestines. The people beat on the gongs and tom-toms, telling the evil spirits that their place of reigning is now over for a time in this village.

We wonder, *Where are we? Who are we?* We feel dazed with the horror of it all. Oh, the darkness of these poor people!

So we preach the message of the true sacrifice of the great Son of God — of His Atonement on Calvary's cross and of the power of His precious blood.

It is not easy to convert these tribespeople away from their beloved gongs and dramatic sacrifices, the feasts and superstitions. When will these cries and wails of fear be changed to hosannas and psalms of praise to the true God? When will these vast stretches of territory, still claimed by Satan, be taken for Christ? Truly this takes the moving power of the Holy Spirit of God!

And before we left Son Ha on this trip, God did work a miracle! Two young Hrey tribesmen believed, simply and joyously praying to God, through Jesus Christ, accepting His great Sacrifice on Calvary's cross and His eternal salvation. God had laid His hands upon them. Their names are Reo and Troi. They, too, were pleased to return with us to Da Nang to study God's Word, along with the Cua young people. Some day these Hreys would return to their people to help spread the Message of Life. Today, seven years later, Reo is one of the faithful Hrey preachers to his own tribe.

We now had another important center of the Hrey tribe to visit — Gi Liang, situated in a Hrei valley, eight miles away from Son Ha. We took our seven Cua and Hrey young people with us, packed in with Anh Hai in the back of the Land Rover pickup.

In Gi Liang we visited the head tribal chief of the district in his fine longhouse built up high from the ground.

Then we stood right beside the sacrifice pole in the center of the village and preached with the flannelgraphs. The people crowded around and some said, "If we'd heard of Christ's sacrifice before, we wouldn't sacrifice the animals."

Others cried, "If what you say about Jesus and His love for us is true, how is it that you white people have not come to tell us before? It is hard for us to change, now that we are old men."

Others asked, "Who is He? Where is He now? Does He care about us Hrey?"

It took some time for them to learn the name of Jesus.

"How do you say it? Tell us again."

"How do I begin to pray to God?"

"How is it that this Vietnamese, Anh Hai, can live with you strange white people all the time and not be bewitched?"

As they saw Anh Hai with us and helping us, it helped them to have confidence in us.

The new young tribal Christians gave their first words of testimony for Christ.

Some of the villagers said, "We want to travel the same road as you — the road to heaven."

Our hearts rejoiced as several young men willingly knelt before God for the first time and followed us, sentence by sentence, as we prayed.

▶ 8 ◀

Headquarters and Bible School

BY NOW, OPERATION SERVICE was approved and authorized as a missionary society by the government of Viet Nam. Gordon was granted a special audience with the President of Viet Nam at that time, Mr. Ngo Dinh Diem. Gordon had written him fully about our desire to evangelize the tribes. He received Gordon cordially in his palace at Saigon and assured him of his interest, saying to go ahead with our program. "You have perfect liberty of action," were his words. He hoped soon to build roads into the interior so that wilder tribes might be civilized.

The President was a devout Roman Catholic but he was favorable to Protestant missions, especially to those which would do some social and medical work.

God now answered more of our prayers and sent us a fine Vietnamese pastor to open up the great Hrey tribal center at Son Ha. This worker would also open up the Gi Liang center. He was Mr. Khiem, who had not had a pastorate for ten years but was eager now to work for God among this new tribe of people. Mr. Khanh and Mr. Ky, our two teachers, highly recommended him.

Gordon negotiated with the government officials for permission to put Mr. Khiem and his family in Son Ha. Government papers with permission were freely granted and Gordon drove Mr. Khiem, his wife and children to Son Ha, where he rented a little Vietnamese shack for them on the main road of the town.

Mr. Khiem was on fire for God and began eagerly to evangelize immediately. He soon had won three more young Hrey men to the Lord and sent them in to our Bible School to study God's Word, making five from that tribe, so far, in our school.

Then God sent us a fine Vietnamese worker and his wife for the Tra Bong center among the Cua tribe. They were Mr. and Mrs. Hap, an older couple, 60 years of age, who had been deep Christians for years. Mr. Hap had been a well-to-do farmer, but now he had heard the call of God for out-and-out service to these tribespeople. He divided all his land among his children, and he and his wife went to man this vitally important place. Gordon received government permission and was able to rent a house for them next to the market where the Cuas come in daily with their products to sell. The government even granted us, immediately, a fine site of land, free of charge, beside this market place, where we could build a chapel and a home for the Vietnamese workers. When Long and Quang, and the three young women, our Cua Christians, had finished their year of Bible School in Da Nang, they would return to help Mr. and Mrs. Hap sow the seed in Tra Bong.

God was quickly doing great things for us. Next to our back-yard there was another property with a good house that had been occupied by the head of the French Military Police. He and all his officers had now moved out of this house and property in August, as the French Military were leaving Viet Nam, and now we were able to rent it and move in. Besides a good, roomy bungalow, there was a long row of outside rooms which we could use as students' rooms for our Bible School, chapel, classroom, dining room and kitchen. There were toilet facilities and six strong prison cells which had been used for Viet Minh Communists. They would now make good storerooms for us. There was a well and a tall cement water tank with an electric pump. In addition to this, the grounds were spacious. The Lord was enabling us to rent this now, but we hoped to be able to purchase it as our main head-quarters in Da Nang.

There was a lot of cleaning, painting and fixing to be done, but we hired Vietnamese workmen and in two weeks everything was in shape.

Our kitchen is outside and our meals are prepared on a brick charcoal stove, with a tin oven placed over the coals. We use a pressure cooker for tough meats.

By now we had many other pets, as the people kept bringing

Top: Mission headquarters bungalow (an old French home) at Da Nang, Viet Nam.
Below: Chesty the Bushman has a friendly visit with one of the Bible school students; Argus pheasant on veranda of headquarters bungalow.

Top: Chesty gets a drink at the tap; Gordon Smith and the lovely, gentle Argus pheasant.
Below: The pet Argus pheasant, a soft cocoa-brown, flecked with lavender dots, with a pure white downy crest.

Top left: Quaint Blue Langur monkey. These do not live long in captivity because they require certain jungle leaves which we do not know about.
Right: Gordon Smith and Ha-Ho, pet Rheusus monkey.
Below: Hop-a-long, the Gibbon ape, rests flat on his back while little tribesgirl pulls on his arm.

Top: Gordon and tame Civet Cat, which looks much like a racoon; Chesty and tribeswoman.
Below: Civet Cat with "Mimi" and "Jo-Jo" in background watching him lap up the milk they mischievously spilled.

them to us as gifts. We have a wonderful Mynah bird from Tra Bong — a glorious songster, who greets the dawn with a concert. He can also talk English very clearly, and calls out in a voice exactly like my own, "Hello, Laura," "Hello, dear," "Bad boy!" He is a glossy, purple-black bird with a black velvet head, and a yellow velvet head-trimming like a cowl, and a bright orange-red beak.

One day I lost my Mynah bird. We searched for him and found that he had been stolen and was now in the squalid backyard of an Arab man in town. I went over to see him and he was all dirty, even his beak was black, but he called out cheerily to me, "Hello, Laura! Hello, dear!" and everyone knew he was my bird. I went to take him away with me, but the Arab said, "You must pay one hundred piastres for him now" (over $1.00).

"But he is my bird," I cried. "Oh, no! You lost him!" he reminded me. "He does not belong to you anymore."

I had to buy him back again for the hundred piastres. It seemed wrong reasoning to me.

We also have a quaint gray and black striped civet cat that looks like a racoon. He has brilliant, brown, night-seeing eyes with bushy light-gray eyebrows. His fur is thick and soft and he has a long black tail. His legs are short and he runs swiftly, smelling close to the ground. Now and then he gives forth a musky smell.

We always have some Rhesus monkeys with their strangely human, sad, little brown faces looking about 100 years old. They are so cute and amusing! What gymnastic feats they perform. They like us and want us to pet them, but sometimes they chatter and scold at us at a great rate and jump up and down with fury. We had one tame Rhesus called Ha-Ho. He folded his arms, bared his teeth in a smile, and made pathetic little bows to us. He looked just like a sad, little old, wrinkled man in a brown, fur coat.

We have a mother monkey and her baby. The mother, Mi-Mi, wraps her arms around the little monkey, Jo-Jo, and making soft noises in her throat, holds him close to her heart. Jo-Jo often rides around on his mother's back like a jockey. They are always looking out for mischief, of course, so we have to keep them in a cage. If they get out they grab the clothes off the line and tear up the thatched roofs to the two cage-houses. They reach out their little human-like hands to us through the cage bars to be friendly with us.

We had a gorgeous peacock all emerald, blue and bronze, and he was very tame and friendly. He would stand beside me while I ate breakfast and I would give him bread crumbs. He'd walk proudly through our house like a king and lived out in our garden, flying up to roost in our trees at night. He hardly ever went outside of our gate. Quite often he would lift his long tail spreading it out like a great fan, and would shimmer it, with its hundreds of metallic blue eyes gleaming among its glistening bronze plumes. Now and then he would give his loud, raucous call of "Ky-a-wack!"

We also had a nice black and white cat and he and the peacock were great friends. The peacock would put his big curved beak right in the cat's face, until his pompom-crest fell over on the cat's head. The cat would stand as if mesmerized, staring him in the eyes. The peacock didn't peck him. They often ate out of the same dish.

We loved our magnificent peacock and had him many months. Then one day he walked out of our gate and down the road and we never saw him again! Some Vietnamese had quickly grabbed him and likely made a good feast of him! We mourned him deeply.

Some Vietnamese friends gave us a gay colored parrot. He is bright green with a pink breast, gray head and a black collar. He talks in Vietnamese, shrieking out, "I bite! I bite!" and then more softly, "Oh, parrot! ah!" He walks in and out of his cage in our pantry and has chewed up a lot of our soft plastic boxes and nibbled at our plastic dish drainer.

Chi Nga, our house-girl, lavishes a lot of attention on our menagerie. The Vietnamese are experts in the care of birds.

All of these pets bring us much cheer and pleasure.

WAGGONER CHRISTIAN CHURCH

▶ 9 ◀

By Motor Boat to the Katu

WE NOW TOOK OUR first trip in our motor boat. We had bought it second-hand in Saigon, had it shipped up and fixed and put a new 30 horsepower Johnson outboard motor on it. We made a strong trailer to haul it behind our Rover pickup. Now we were ready to take off for the mountains. We have used everything — ox-cart, elephant, plane and jeep — during our twenty-six years out here, but this motor boat was something new for us.

We were going to a section of the Katu tribe which was of a different dialect from the Katu we had visited up on the mountain-top near Da Nang, in the village of Lo-O. These other Katu were farther west and south of Da Nang, near the frontier Vietnamese trading post of Thanh My and as yet there was no road into these mountains. They could only be reached by river boat.

Gordon had already been up to Thanh My, traveling by hired sampan, to scout out the land. It had taken him three days to get there, rowing a mile an hour against the strong current. Now we were so thankful to God that He had provided us with this strong, fast little launch through gifts from friends in America.

We hauled the cream and blue boat on its trailer over to the Da Nang River a few yards from our house, and launched it for its first trip up the rivers, to penetrate back into the mountains to visit the wild Katu.

It was early morning as we moved up the river with Anh Hai and our Cua student, Quang, on board. We had a big load of gasoline with us, our bedding rolls and food. The boat was 14 feet long, made of heavy hardwood, and we had made a canvas top with side curtains for it.

66

Through a misty rain we threaded among sampans and huge square fishing nets which were lowered and raised by pulleys from little platforms in the shallow river. There was such a maze of turns and side streams that, although Gordon followed a good map, we soon found ourselves on the wrong branch. We got back on course after using up half an hour's gas.

Late in the afternoon we reached Ai Nghai only about forty miles along the way. We had used up too much gas against the strong current to risk going into the interior without adding to our supply. So we docked at Ai Nghai and slept in a little Vietnamese shack. Next morning Gordon took a native bus back to Da Nang to fetch our car and trailer and another load of gas. It took him most of the day because of terrible roads. Quang, Anh Hai and I witnessed for the Lord to the Vietnamese people in the little shacks of Ai Nghai and some were open to the Gospel.

Early the following day we set off in the boat again. The river was so shallow in places that we churned up the sandy bottom many times. We had to follow the deepest water around the longest, widest swings of the river and of course the current was strongest there. So we could not cut corners to make good time.

It was pleasant chugging merrily along through the vistas of flat, green farms, with innumerable little figures of Vietnamese men and women under their large cone-shaped hats bending, hoeing and planting their crops of rice, peanuts, manioc and sweet potatoes. The country is full of bamboo thatched huts and villages nestling in among clusters of coconut and bamboo trees. What great numbers of people to reach with the Gospel! Always there were the mat-roofed sampans and rafts of logs and bamboo, drifting past us down the river. The water lapped against the banks and the current gurgled. The slopes rose ever higher and soon mountains with crags and peaks pierced the sky above us. White lacy waterfalls poured off the cliffs with a mellow hum.

At noon we arrived at the village of Dai An where we stopped to visit a district administrator to tell him our plans of visiting the Katu mountaineers. These tribes are often called "the Blood-hunters" because they sometimes make human sacrifices. Our goal

Top: Katu tribespeople visit motor boat. The two little boys helped carry luggage.
Below: Katu tribespeople see their first white woman.

Top: Tribespeople in mountaintop village of Mo-O across the river from Thanh My.
Below: Chief's house in Mo-O.

Left: Gordon with two Katu warriors.

Below: Katu tribespeople gather around the author and her husband as they eat their evening meal. The people didn't like the bread and jam, but they did like canned meat and sardines.

Right: Katu tribespeople of Bong Bok, unsubdued by Vietnamese government. Many are now following the communists.
Below: Katu tribeswoman with back basket of gourds for water.

of Thanh My was the last group of Vietnamese huts in the tribal territory ahead.

As we churned on against the ever stronger swirling stream, we ate our dinner in the launch, appreciating some special kind treats out of parcels from home.

By three o'clock we reached Thanh My, the last little Vietnamese settlement, all alone among the Katu villages surrounding it. The Vietnamese family from a hut where Gordon had camped the time before, recognized him and they came rushing down the river bank to welcome us. How excited they were to see the motor boat and they invited us to stay in their house again.

The first night we preached to a good crowd of Vietnamese who came from their little shacks along the river bank. Quang, the Cua student, explained the Gospel in Vietnamese from our picture rolls and both Gordon and I could now give short messages in the tonal Vietnamese language.

The next morning we took a woven bamboo sampan across the river to visit some Katu tribespeople, who were coming down from their village of Mo-O, high up on the steep mountain, to exchange betel vine leaves for rice. Gordon had visited this wild village when he was here before and had photographed some of the people. As our sampan pulled up to the bank, I saw some of the very people we had gazed at in the snapshots. My heart leaped and I was greatly touched to meet them face to face.

They had been rather hostile when Gordon visited them up in their village that first time, but now they seemed pleased to see him again and to see me, the first white woman they had ever met. They remembered that Gordon had promised them that I would come and they clustered around us, laughing and chattering, very interested in my red and blue striped pullover and my glasses. Their copper-brown bodies were almost naked — the men wear loin-cloths, and the women a short piece of cloth used as a wrap-around skirt. The men had their hair done in a knob at the back caught with a fancy wooden comb, tassels of beads, and some with a great curved boar's tusk. They had collars of white and red beads hanging in long dangles down their backs, as well as bracelets and anklets. Some young men had brass rings encircling their hips. They carried long spears.

We gave out some medicines to them, malaria pills and aureomycine ointment for sore eyes, and some clothing to keep them warm at night. Gordon took Polaroid photos of them. On his previous visit they had been much afraid and angry when he "caught them in his magic box — the Rolleiflex — with the eye that pointed at them." But now as they looked at the pictures Gordon had brought to show them, they laughed to see themselves, but they still refused to accept them. They asked our Vietnamese host, who was a trader among these Katu people, to keep the photos for them in his house across the river. They found they had no ill effects from Gordon's taking photos of them before, so now they were gradually losing some of their fear.

Quang preached the gospel message to them from the picture-rolls and gave his testimony as a converted Cua tribesman. They listened with great attention to this fellow mountaineer.

That afternoon quite a crowd of other Katu from this same village of Mo-O came over to the Vietnamese house to visit with us. We gave out clothing to them also and witnessed to them of Christ.

At night we had another large meeting at the house with crowds of interested Vietnamese farmers.

The following morning we set out with Vietnamese guides for a Katu village called Bong Bok, which was two miles away from our camp. Gordon had visited this village also on his previous trip and had found the people friendly.

We followed a trail winding through tall grass in the mountain valley. Some of this trail was the remains of an old road the French had built through this country years ago, leading to the fort of Ben Giang, which they had established on the frontier of this wild Katu country.

We ourselves had followed this road eighteen years before, by car to Ben Giang, and had been greatly challenged by these Katu bloodhunters. We had been able to send in a Vietnamese evangelist who began preaching the Gospel among them. Then came the fifteen years of war. The road was abandoned and the bridges and fort had all been destroyed by the Viet Minh Communists. Nothing was left now but this scarcely discernible footpath through the jungle. The tropical forest soon reclaims any space left to it. But we heard the good news that the Vietnamese government now intended to rebuild this road with American aid money and equipment, and it would reach from Thanh My, where we were now camping, back through the forest and mountains to Kontum, two hundred miles away to the South. This would open a vast interior to missionary work.

Trudging the jungle trail, Gordon and I were back in our elements again, wading clear streams, crossing ravines on rickety poles. Peacocks gave their loud call near our trail and there were fresh tiger tracks a dozen times right in our pathway. I was glad that Gordon had his loaded gun and our eyes were trained for a glimpse of a yellow coat with black stripes or the black rosettes of a leopard in the tall grasses. It was exciting and frightening to be right in the thick of tiger country, but we also knew we were in the care of God.

We passed the remains of an abandoned village and Gordon recognized it as the very place where Bong Bok had been when he had visited it a few weeks previously. Now the "evil-spirits" of sickness and death had entered the village and in fear, they had moved their houses away to a new site.

The barking of dogs and crowing of roosters told us that we were now nearing the cluster of new houses and our guides began to shout, "We come! We come!" and to cough, to let them know who we were. This was the Katu's polite way of ringing the doorbell. Enemies would creep up silently.

As we climbed over the fence into the village, I was surprised to see how good these Katu longhouses were — seven or eight oblong bamboo houses built up on stilts and arranged in a circle around a compound. In the center of the enclosure was the fancy carved pole used for tying up the water-buffaloes for the animal sacrifices.

Crowds of brown men, women and children poured out of their houses to see us. They had masses of dark hair hanging loose or done up in knobs decorated with pompoms of beads. Some wore bangs hanging down to their eyes. They had big wooden discs in their ear lobes. The women wore short, skimpy skirts and some had a halter bib for a blouse.

They all remembered Gordon and his good medicines on his last trip and the chief ushered us into his longhouse. They were pleased that I had come to visit them, too — the first white woman they had ever seen.

The chief's house was one room, thirty feet long by fifteen feet wide. The roof was high, sloping down from a center ridge-pole and was neatly thatched with finely woven pandanus leaves. At each circular end of the room was a family stove — a block of hard earth with a wood fire built around three stones, and a blackened clay cook-pot boiling on top. The floor was elastic lattices of bamboo. There were stacks of firewood, bamboo tubes filled with water, hand-woven back-baskets and trays. The bronze gongs used for the sacrificial ceremonies were piled up on a shelf. A big drum was suspended from the ceiling and long spears and knives were stuck in the roof.

There were two good hammocks of bamboo and strong rattan ropes, and I sat down in one as we visited with the crowds of people who swarmed in, laughing, shouting and staring at us. Gordon sat in the middle of the bamboo floor making good contacts by doctoring sore eyes and giving out pieces of clothing from friends in America. The chief was soon resplendent in a woman's bright green short coat, and his wife in a sweater from Elkhart, Indiana!

Then we heated a can or two of food on one of the fireplaces and ate our supper with the crowd of tribespeople milling around us.

Later as our hosts sat around their evening meal, and as we visited around in the circle of longhouses, we were shocked to see that these people had nothing to eat but a bowl of boiled green papaya fruit for each adult and a thin soup of rice for the children. One or two of them had been so kind as to offer us a bowl of rice which, perhaps, would have been their last if we had taken it! They told us that their last crop had been destroyed by drought, marauding wild elephants and wild pigs. They had just planted some corn but until it ripened they had little but roots and leaves to eat. The bit of rice they did have, had been obtained by exchanging heavy loads of betel leaves with the Vietnamese at Thanh My.

We discovered that many other of the Katu villages in this section were on starvation rations in the same way, through crop failures.

We planned that when we returned home to Da Nang we'd arrange with government officials to have some American relief food shipped by sampan to these people immediately.

The Katu that night responded to the gospel songs and messages with much interest, peering in awe at the picture-rolls we showed of Christ. Two young men were outstanding. They were elegant in their fancy headdress — big hair-buns held with carved wooden combs, curved boars' tusks, and tassels of red and white beads hanging down their backs. They had discs of tin in their ear-lobes and collars of beads and dark blue loin-cloths. They were interested in the testimony of Quang, the Cua tribesman, and to hear that he and other young tribespeople were staying in Da Nang with us, studying God's Word. They cried, "Oh, if we were to leave our homes and go so far away the spirits would make us sick and die. We could never think of going with you." They greatly fear the outside world.

After the meeting, we found a place in the room where we could spread our bedding-rolls on the bamboo floor and hang up our mosquito nettings. The fires in the circular ends of the room were burning brightly and it was cozy in the firelight.

The crowd watched our every movement, trying to peer through our khaki army mosquito nets to see us getting ready for bed in the shelter of our bed rolls. When Gordon stepped out in gay striped pajamas, they laughed and cheered with admiration. Just owning two changes of clothing would be a fortune to them, for few of them even owned a shirt. They wondered why Gordon didn't wear such a fine suit in the daytime! They made a wall as they sat around our nets far into the night, smoking their long, hand-rolled cigars and bamboo pipes. It was hard to sleep with all their talking, the clouds of smoke, their terrible fits of coughing and spitting. Every now and then someone would call out to a neighboring house and there would be talking back and forth. Some messages would be relayed on to other houses in the circle. The old chief hardly slept all night and he kept the fire by his bed-mat, near mine, burning bright and warm. Others in the longhouse snored powerfully. We did not need to worry any about thieving as the tribespeople consider their visitors sacred.

Before dawn the household was astir making fires and the roosters made more sleep impossible.

Anh Hai had bought four eggs from the Katu for our breakfast and boiled them, but we found they had seen better days. The chief's children enjoyed them, however. Our canned butter was rancid and our bread from Da Nang was now mildewed. The chief kindly offered us his tea bowl, but he had been sipping from it himself through the night. Even so, we had much more to be thankful for than these poor people with only their thin watery soup to eat. And this would have to do them through the whole day!

We spent the morning visiting in all the circle of houses. The people were busy now, young and old, rolling up betel leaves in packages to take to Thanh My to exchange for a few bowls of rice which would be especially for their children.

When the sun rose higher we took photos, the two well-formed young fellows in festive attire being the only ones willing to have their pictures taken on the Polaroid. Going into their houses, they brought out their bows and arrows and sharp, curved knives and did a war dance for us. They danced around each other, making high jumps, plunging to hit low, feinting, with their shields before them, using their knives with rapid dexterity (the Katu learn to fight from childhood). They were delighted when we showed them photos of themselves taken by the Polaroid.

Back at Thanh-My we went by sampan up the river and saw another group of Katu working in their field plots on the river bank and we called out to them as we passed by. The copper-colored men were dressed only in their loin-cloths and heavy necklaces of white beads.

In our closing night meeting at Thanh My our host and his wife and boys and another Vietnamese knelt down and gave their hearts to the Lord Jesus. We were thrilled over and over to hear our dear Cua student, Quang, witnessing continually to the people. He, himself, had only known of Christ a few months, but he had truly cut clean from his old heathen ways and we knew he was going to make a fine preacher. His was a very sweet spirit.

Early next morning, before we set out for home, we purchased our host's house for about forty dollars, as a temporary place for a Vietnamese missionary. We felt sure that God would send us a worker soon for this strategic center among the Katu tribe and these back-country Vietnamese.

Shortly afterward, God did answer our faith and sent us a worker for this district, Mr. Phuong. He was formerly a preacher in North Viet Nam, but for the last ten years during the war, he had had no ministry and was making a living cutting timber in the jungle in this Katu country. He came to us saying he had a burden to preach to the Katu and since he knew many of them and their ways of life, we took him on and placed him in Thanh My. He immediately threw himself wholeheartedly into the work.

We sped down the current in half the time it took us to go up and despite rain at times, we revelled in the purple and green mountains with clouds like snow-white layers of cotton wool lying low over them. At noon our boat pulled into the shore of Ai Nghai.

Now some difficult hours lay ahead of us. It had been raining here in a violent deluge while we were away and the roads were in a frightful condition. I could hardly scramble up the slippery bank of mire. It was a gruelling task for Gordon to back the Rover and boat-trailer down the steep, slippery road bank and get the launch winched up with a cable on to its trailer.

Then came the trip down eight miles of terrible road. It had been almost impassable before the rains, but now the Vietnamese of the village warned us that we could never make it. They said that our narrow Land Rover and heavy launch at the back of it could never get through the deep ruts and slippery mud. We'd tip over into the ditches and the wet rice fields.

But with courage Gordon set his teeth and decided to try it. Off we went over deep holes and quagmires, slipping and sliding. I'd shut my eyes and cry to God as Gordon would attempt furrows and trenches that seemed impossible. Crashing, bumping through deep gutters, mud and water flying, we ploughed through and the Rover and boat, somehow, stayed upright. My nerves were so taut and shaken when we finished the last and worst stretch at the end of the eight miles, that I burst into tears.

How thankful and relieved we were to get through! The lovely cream and blue boat and yellow trailer were a mass of mud, but nothing had been hurt. It was a great relief to hit the hard pavement of the main highway again. By four o'clock we were home once more with the monkeys and gibbons calling out their welcome.

Nearly a week had passed on this trip to Thanh My and we were elated with the open hearts of the people there, the challenge and good prospects ahead. We prayed that some day pioneer white missionaries would take up this task along with the Vietnamese evangelist at Thanh My.

WAGGONER CHRISTIAN CHURCH

▶ 10 ◀

The Pakoh and Baru

SIXTY MILES NORTH OF Da Nang, and six miles west of the city of Hue, is the jumping-off place for the Pakoh tribe reaching over to Laos; and forty miles north of Hue, and fifteen miles west of the city of Quang Tri, just eleven miles from the 17th Parallel, is the great Baru tribe.

We must lose no time in doing our part to bring Christ to these unreached places in Central Viet Nam.

Outside of the city of Hue is a little market place called Bang Lang and the Pakoh tribespeople come in here to trade. Here we would be able to reach this wild, neglected tribe, living back in the untouched mountain jungles, unvisited by white men.

The trip from Da Nang to Hue is one of the most scenic in all of Viet Nam. A good macadamized highway, which is the old Mandarin Road, climbs from the sea-coast up the mountains to a height of 1450 feet at the "Col de Nuages" — the "Pass in the Clouds."

As we slowly wound up the steep road cut from the mountain side, our hearts feasted upon the marvelous beauty of the vast open sea below, shading through blues, greens, lilacs, purples and sparkling in the sunlight like a floor of jewels out to the horizon. Hundreds of sampans with their yellow sails moved on the face of it, no bigger than toys from this height.

To the left of us lie the matted jungle mountain slopes, vivid green, towering to the sky. The trees, bushes and rocks are entwined and festooned with vines, some varieties having masses of white, bell-like blooms, others having yellow and purple clusters.

Up at the "Pass in the Clouds," the high mountains roll back

in tiers on either side and one can look out, first on one side
and then on the other, far down to the miles of curving sea-
beaches and the broad expanse of the ocean as far as the eye
can see.

At this Pass the one-way traffic comes up the mountain from
both sides and meets on top, and there for half an hour one waits
until all the straggling trucks, buses, taxis, private cars, and especially the big military vehicles arrive.

Vietnamese people from their little restaurants come to our cars
with something to sell — sweetened lotus-seed drink, fruit, hot
steamed rice-flour dumplings, with bits of fat pork inside, peanuts,
hot tea. Or we can go into the restaurant shacks and have bitter
black coffee with sweetened condensed milk, or orange and sars-
parilla pop — or even a coke!

Then when a whistle blows, everyone takes off on either side
of the mountain, going down faster than they came up. Some
make it a dangerous race, and sometimes there are accidents on
the hairpin curves.

The city of Hue was the Emperors' capital of Viet Nam from
the year 1820 until 1954 — the residence of the Emperors. It was
old Viet Nam, with its courteous speech and gracious manners.
The women of Hue, today, are especially distinguished in their
manners and carriage, because of the long association of their town
with royalty.

In Hue, we of the Protestant faith meet much sophisticated
resistance to the Gospel. The city is strong in the Buddhist faith.
The Buddhists are just as cold toward the Gospel of Christ, in
their cultured way, as the wild, brown savages up in the unsubdued tribal villages back in the jungle mountains. The Hue
people are charming, courteous, always bowing, smiling, dignified
and apologetic, but adamant against the true Gospel. We bring
them a new message, different from Buddhism, Confucianism and
Taoism. For decades the Christian and Missionary Alliance have
had a struggling church in Hue.

On our first visit to Bang Lang, near the Minh Mang tomb, we
met the Pakoh tribespeople, wandering around the little Vietnamese market. Only a few miles separate the cultured Vietnamese
of Hue from the almost naked jungle-dwellers who come to Bang

Lang. In fact, these tribes sometimes come in to the Hue market itself. Their only touch with civilization is the Vietnamese market where they like to trade their rattan, deer horns and wild honey for kerosene lanterns, cigarette lighters, a shirt or two, and Vietnamese rice alcohol.

Besides having their own age-old culture, the Vietnamese have been under the French civilization for one hundred years, but these tribespeople, living back in their forests, are the same wild people today as they were thousands of years ago, back in time unknown. They are practically untouched by civilization. They do not know their age. They do not know years, or months or hours. They count by ten fingers and the knots on a string. Their language had never been put into writing. They, like nearly all the other tribes in the Central Viet Nam mountains, had never had any medicine, teachers or schools, and they had never had one ray of gospel light.

We heard that a great number of these Pakoh tribespeople had just been brought down to Bang Lang by the Vietnamese government for a big political rally that would last three or four days. The government had invited them to come in to try to win their allegiance, for they are still unsubdued. They would be given meat and rice and some presents of cloth, combs, soap, coils of copper, mirrors, knives, tobacco and salt. They were camping across the river under tents put up for them by the Administration. Nearby, on a grassy hillside, six or seven of their elephants were browsing. Some of the tribespeople had ridden on elephant back six days' journey from the West.

We decided to stay over in Bang Lang for a couple of days to visit with these tribespeople, so we found a little Vietnamese shack in which to camp.

Crossing the river in a sampan we came to the big encampment of over a thousand of the wild Pakoh people! They were squatting on their haunches around their smoky wood fires and baskets. We eagerly went from tent to tent visiting among them. It was surprising to see that they tattoo their faces, chests and arms with all sorts of blue figures — suns, moons, stars and crosses. They all pluck out their eyebrows to a fine line — some even pluck them clean away and tattoo new eyebrows, reaching back to the ears, in a blue design — some of dots and some of stars!

Their costumes are somewhat different from the other tribes we know. The women wear a long, loose open-necked shirt in dark blue and red striped homespun. Their skirts of the same cloth reach to their knees. Most of the men were naked except for a loin-cloth and some had a red and blue blanket hanging over a shoulder. They do their hair with a fringe in front and a knob at the back — but some of them just left their tangled, dirty, bushy hair hanging loose to their shoulders. They all have their top front teeth sawed off close to their gums like most of the other tribes in Viet Nam. Large pewter rings hang from their ears. Around their necks are a profusion of beads, chains and old silver coins. Some women were carrying babies in cloth slings on their backs, and there were naked, tousled children standing around.

They are an exceedingly poor people, hungry and full of sickness and dark superstitions.

The Vietnamese Administrator of Bang Lang, for these mountaineer people, showed us on his map 103 villages back in these mountains where there are 13,000 of these poor Pakoh people. The villages can only be reached by foot, with from two to five days climbing hard mountains to get to them. It will take strongwinded, young pioneer missionaries to work this hard field.

We would have to wait until the close of our Bible School's first year term in June, before we would have a Vietnamese worker to put in this center for the Pakoh. In the meantime, we, ourselves, would drive up as frequently as possible and sometimes, during week-ends, bring some of the Bible students with us to help witness. It seemed a miraculous working of God that we were able to find a little bamboo hut that we could rent and so have a base for "Operation Service" in Bang Lang.

Our next place to open for the Gospel was among the Baru tribe, 55 miles to the north and west of Hue. Again we followed the coastal highway, driving through some stretches of plain scrub country that looked like pasture land. The purple mountains lie on the horizon about ten miles away. By the roadside is the ubiquitous sensitive plant with mauve balls of downy flowers that look

Top: In the garden of the Tomb of Min Mang at Hue — old Vietnamese Emperor of 1840.
Below: Tomb of Khai Dinh, the father of deposed Emperor Bao Dai of today.

Baru girl of Van Kiu tribe, Quang Tri province. Notice tattoo marks on forehead and around the chin.

Left: Baru tribesgirl at market-place in Cam Phu. Notice rows of silver coins from earlier days which decorate her blouse.
Below: Another Baru tribesgirl. Notice Laotian style hairdo.

like mimosa. If touched, the stalk will droop and all the leaves will close up tightly. Even the vibration of our approaching car would be enough to wilt these hypersensitive leaves. There were eucalyptus trees recently planted by the government along some of the way. They are tall, graceful trees with an aromatic scent. And then there are broad stretches of rice fields spreading out as far as the eye can see.

The city of Quang Tri is the center of this province of the same name. The town of Dong Ha is a few miles farther on and here, just about eleven miles from the 17th Parallel that marks the border of Communist North Viet Nam, we turned off, straight west, on the good highway that goes over to Savannaket, Laos.

The first Baru houses appeared after we traveled about fifteen miles. These people number 50,000, including some members of the tribe over in Laos and some above the 17th Parallel in North Viet Nam.

On this first trip we drove right through to the important Baru tribal center of Khe Sanh, a few miles from the Laotian border. The Christian and Missionary Alliance began work here in this center in 1931. Then the work was interrupted and largely dispersed during the war years. Now a Vietnamese couple, who used to work with us among the tribes at Banmethuot, Mr. and Mrs. Loc, had just been stationed here under the C. and M. A., and they are reaching the thickly populated section of tribal villages in the Khe Sanh area.

We found that there was a big gap now to be filled in among this tribe, thirty miles back along the road toward the coast. We agreed with Mr. and Mrs. Loc that we would open a strategic center for the Baru in this area at a little Vietnamese market village called Cam Phu. There were 10,000 Baru here who had never heard the Gospel. So we clearly felt that God was leading us to enter this section.

Cam Phu is a delightful place. Mountains of limestone rise up vertically out of the valley to a height of several hundred feet, their gray rock half covered with shrubs and small trees. Some of these mountains are like steep cones, the rock shading through to a rough point. Others resemble craggy eminences surmounted by feudal castle ruins; still others are sugar-loaf shapes. One could imagine that magicians, dwarfs, gnomes and elves hide in these mysterious looking abodes.

The Cam Phu village was made up of little Vietnamese huts built of dry clay and thatched roofs, dark inside, all identical. Every few days a market is held in a central place, when trucks come in from the nearest town of Dong Ha and set up display booths of their wares. Vietnamese men and women from little farms and gardens round about also come down the road to the market carrying basket loads at each end of a supple bamboo pole over the shoulder. The pole bends an inch or so in tune with the shuffling jog-trot of its bearer. The people suffer bad callouses of the shoulder bones from this heavy pole-carrying. They bring in fresh vegetables, rice, meat, fish, even live pigs, all trussed up tightly.

The Baru tribespeople also come pouring in from their villages in the mountains. They come to trade their jungle produce for rice, dried fish, eggs, brown sugar, cloth, salt, beads — all things dear to their hearts.

We found the Baru different from any of the other tribes in Viet Nam, with a distinct Laotian aspect because they live so close to the border. The women follow the Laotian style hair-do with a big, tight, spiral knob over to one side of the head and a colored cloth turban in a roll like a crown around her head, having one loose end hanging down the back. They wear the colorful, long Laotian skirt with a wide border of aluminum thread design. Rows of silver coins like big buttons decorate the front of their vests and their long necklaces are loaded with more dangling silver coins from an earlier epoch. They have long earrings sometimes caught with fine chains that loop from ear to ear under their chins.

Like the Pakoh tribe, tattooing is also a popular custom among these Baru people and nearly all have small mystic symbols on their faces. They also have the fearful custom of having their six upper front teeth cut off at the gums at the age of puberty.

We scouted around and found a little bamboo hut that we could rent for a Vietnamese worker who would come in to open up this center to the Gospel.

As we returned to Da Nang we found that God had answered our prayers and sent us a fine Vietnamese couple for this place — Mr. and Mrs. Kinh and their family of five children. They had received Bible School training and had witnessed much for God in their local church. Now they felt the Lord was calling them out to take the name of Christ to this great unreached section of the Baru tribe, and also the many back-country Vietnamese around this center who were without the Gospel. We moved them up to Cam Phu immediately and they began a good work for the Lord there.

In a few months' time a number of Vietnamese and several Baru tribespeople had believed in Christ. Gifts came in from kind, faithful friends in the homeland and a new bamboo chapel and preacher's house were soon built in this center.

► 11 ◄
Forging Ahead

EARLY IN 1957 OUR National Church Committee was formed with Mr. Khanh, Mr. Ky, Mr. Nhut and Gordon. A Vietnamese name for the Society was chosen, "Co Doc Truyen Giao Hoi," which means literally, "Society for the Propagation of Christianity." A French lawyer helped draw up a constitution which was presented to the government.

In order to incorporate our mission with the government, we were required to establish an Administrative Council with a Vietnamese director and at least two-thirds of the members Vietnamese. When the names on this Committee were submitted to the government, they were approved and thus our new National Church came into being as an incorporated society. Mr. Nhut was Director, and he, with Mr. Phuong and Gordon, made up this Administrative Council, whose function was to represent the mission to the government. The main advantage of incorporation was to facilitate the purchase of property which always has to be in the name of a Vietnamese society.

At this time we received a letter from a former Christian and Missionary Alliance Vietnamese preacher, Mr. Lich, who, in the past, had worked for five years with the Cham race of people in the south. He now asked to join our mission to work among the Central tribes. Mr. Lich was at that time running his own sawmill at the mountain resort of Dalat, as it had been some time since a ministry had been offered to him under his own mission. He was making good money in this work, but was ready now to forsake all of this for the Lord's work.

Friends of Mr. Lich highly recommended him to us, so we

asked him to come and he began a most fruitful ministry with us. He was destined to become one of the most important members of our mission.

For some months now we had been wanting to open up Bato and Gia Vuc, the great Hrey tribal section next to Son Ha. Mr. Lich felt the call of God to be the first evangelist to settle in this area and to give his full time to the work of spreading the Gospel among the tens of thousands of Hrey tribespeople and also among the many Vietnamese in that area.

We drove Mr. Lich from Da Nang down the coastal highway. We passed by the now familiar side roads going in to Tra Bong and Son Ha, where Mr. and Mrs. Hap and Mr. and Mrs. Khiem were working, and went on twenty miles beyond Quang Ngai to the Vietnamese town of Mo Duc. Here we turned off on a road leading westward into the great valley of Bato surrounded by towering mountains. Our trip was the first visit a missionary had ever made into this section. As on the other side trails, the road in the twenty miles from the coast was extremely rough, but the authorities were expecting to repair it soon. It led back beyond Bato and Gia Vuc to meet a new road leading to Son Ha and Gi Liang, thus linking up all these important Hrey centers.

Another strategic road was being built with American aid, zig-zagging steeply up 2,600 feet from the plains of Bato and Gia Vuc, going west into the high mountains of Plateau G.I. and on to Kontum. There it would join the main highway being pushed north through Dak To, Dak Sut, Dak Pek and Dak Ro-tah, leading to Thanh My and around to Da Nang again — a wonderful link to all these future mission stations!

This great Circle Route, when completed, would take us through many unreached tribes — the Hrey, Monom, Bahnar, Sedang, Halang, Jeh and Katu. What an opportunity for full-scale missionary endeavor of every kind!

It was thrilling to come to this magnificent valley of Bato, the capital of the Hrey. It stretched before us like an Eden with its shining Bato River winding through bright green rice fields, well-cultivated in terraces; the Hrey villages of longhouses nestling in the dark verdure of graceful areca-nut palms and bamboo; and the

Top: Katu tribesmother and children. Even the children smoke pipes!
Right: Katu warrior of Go village. Notice sharp curved knife and hand-
painted wooden shield.
Below: Laura and Gordon Smith hire sampans for their load of American relief food (rice, beans, and clothing, too) for trip upriver to dis-
tribute among Katu at Thanh My and beyond.

Right: Preaching at the dedication service of the chapel at Bato, using the flannelgraph lesson, "The Two Remedies" (Moses' serpent in the wilderness and Christ's death on the cross).

Below: Archway and flag at Bato dedication.

Top: Anh Hai, the cook, at left in felt hat, and Katu porters.
Below: A Katu family, man with spear to protect from tigers and leopards, mother and daughter smoking pipes.

Top: Katu boys. Notice safety pin necklaces.
Below: Katu people starting out for rice fields on mountainside. Notice long spears for protection from leopards and tigers.

mighty mountains looming up, blue and violet, on either side and rolling far away into the distance down the valley.

The Hrey people are proud of these fertile valleys of Bato, Gia Vuc, Son Ha and Gi-Liang. It is warm in the valleys which lie at sea-level. Most of the tribespeople of Viet Nam have to live up in the cold, rainy mountains, where they often have little to eat.

Gordon and Mr. Lich visited the Administrator in the Vietnamese settlement of Bato and were able to get a fine piece of land for our mission, about two acres in size, on the main road, just outside the town.

It was a beautiful site for a mission center, on a rise of land that overlooked the whole panorama of valley and mountains. Right across the paddy fields, facing the site, lies a great bulk of mountain range, the slopes a huge mosaic with the varied greens of grass and dark jungle blending into the blues and purples of the peaks.

How grateful we were for a special gift for the cost of opening up Bato to the Gospel, which came to us from a faithful group of prayer partners in Chicago. With this gift, Mr. Lich was able to move into Bato and begin to oversee the building of a little mission house for himself and his large family, and a mud-walled and thatched-roof chapel.

A few months later these buildings were dedicated and some, both from the Hrey tribespeople and the Vietnamese, were beginning to come to the Lord. The church in Bato was born. A few tribespeople were forsaking their old animal sacrifices and calling on the demons; and some Vietnamese were renouncing all idolatry, burning up the family gods and the ancestral tablets. They were giving up Taoism, "The Way," which is false, for "The True Way" who had come down from heaven.

One of these new tribal Christians was Ghe, who later entered our Bible School at Da Nang and today is one of the Hrey evangelists working at Bato. A Vietnamese who accepted Christ at that time, Huk, has also attended our Bible School for two years and is now, with his wife and children, out opening a great work for God on the Ly Son Island off the coast.

Soon after the opening of Bato, Gordon and I, on a Sunday afternoon, drove out of Da Nang to explore a little road that led back into the nearby mountains. It was a beautiful ten-mile trip over the hills with a lovely view of the great mountain ranges a few miles to the West, where the Katu tribespeople live.

Arriving at a crowded little market place called Phu Hoa, we were excited to see a number of ill-clad Katu men, women and children mingling with the Vietnamese. They wore long necklaces of large black and white beads with tigers' teeth and claws and the beaks of the horn-bill bird strung here and there among the beads. We spoke to them in Vietnamese and found they came from villages a few miles back in the mountains. They were much friendlier than those first Katu we had visited up on the high mountain top a little to the north.

Not wanting to let them slip through our fingers, we asked them if they would like to go for a ride back with us to Da Nang where we would show them some moving pictures. They seemed quite pleased with the idea, so before long we rolled in to our mission yard with the first load of Katu tribespeople ever to come in contact with our headquarters. We fed them some cookies and candy and then showed them moving pictures of our Raday tribespeople down at Banmethuot. They were very interested to see these fellow tribesmen. Then we showed them some travel pictures of African animals which really thrilled them. When they saw the giraffes, their cries sounded to us as if they were saying, "There ain't no such animal!" They shouted and laughed in their explosive Katu dialect that sounded much like hens cackling. We tried to explain the Gospel to them, using pictures, and later that evening drove them back to Phu Hoa market, with many a handshake and friendly smile on both sides. We promised to visit them in their mountain villages soon.

No Gospel work had ever been done in this area, so we decided that Phu Hoa would be a splendid center from which to reach this particular dialect of the Katu.

To get Phu Hoa opened to the Gospel, we arranged for Mr. Phuong to make visits there from Thanh My from time to time. This meant a hard, long trip of around 45 miles for him by sampan down the Thanh My River and then by bicycle.

Some months previously, we had already sent two Vietnamese women for training to the Hue Hospital for a nursing course of six months. They were Mrs. Thuan and Miss An — the latter being the oldest daughter of Mr. and Mrs. Nhut. As soon as they received their nursing certificates, we placed them at Thanh My and moved Mr. Phuong and his family to Phu Hoa. We rented a little bamboo house for them there and Mr. Phuong began to contact the Katu in this area and made trips to the nearest tribal villages.

One day Gordon took two of our Bible School students, Thuong, the Vietnamese, formerly from Hanoi, and Quang, the Cua student, and with Mr. Phuong, they went out on a long trip far back in these mountains to visit a dozen Katu villages.

It was dangerous going over slimy stones through black-green jungle. There was hardly a rift in the thick canopy of boughs overhead. Gordon always carried his big-game rifle, a 10.75 Mauser, for he felt safer leading the party in single file through the jungle with a good weapon in his hands, as there are many wild animals to be encountered. This is the country of tiger and elephant and it would have afforded marvelous hunting, but the men hadn't the time for it on this trip. Blood-suckers stuck to them, coming from the branches, grass and leaves along the river. Soon the men's faces were sweating and their hearts were pounding.

Back in this village of Balien they visited quite a few of the Katu whom we had met at Phu Hoa market from time to time. They gave Gordon the place of honor to spread out his sleeping bag in their communal house. This was under the altar, above which their sacrificial buffalo heads were hung. More than once, Gordon woke up feeling soft things moving over his face. He found they were just white maggots that were dropping down from the putrifying, odoriforous skulls above!

These Katu seemed interested in the message of the Gospel, but, as among most of the tribes, they'll do "what the chief does." If he believes, they'll also believe, or vice versa. It is hard to get individual decisions. They like to believe by communities. The chief's word carries much weight.

The trip back was made faster and near evening the men arrived at the plateau on top of the ravine after a long day's hike all the way from Balien and the other group of villages. They had expected to pass the night in a village at the ravine's edge but found the place full of Vietnamese soldiers who had come up on patrol against any lurking Communists. Having no room in which to sleep, Gordon and the evangelists started out at dusk for the trip down the steep gorge, taking with them bundles of dried reeds which they would use as torches in the pitch blackness gathering fast. Gordon's flashlight soon gave out and the torches burned up so quickly that most of the time they were slithering down and wading through water in the dark. The men would break off more reeds and light them, but it was hardly enough light to see the way through the dangerous, slippery rocks and rapids. But, at last, stiff and sore, around midnight they reached the Vietnamese village at the bottom of the ravine. They were soon rolled up in their blankets on a bamboo floor, dead to the world.

But not long after, everyone was awakened by the trumpeting of wild elephants a few hundred yards away across the stream. They seemed to be headed for the gardens around the tiny settlement. If a troop of elephants get into a village they soon knock down the bamboo houses, smash up rice bins and utensils and eat up all the banana plants and garden stuffs. All the people rushed out shouting and banging on tin cans to scare the big beasts away. Gordon shot his rifle into the air a few times. Elephants don't like noise and eventually the sound of their trampling and crackling through the bamboo forest gradually died away, but they seemed to take their time about it.

The sampan took the men back to Phu Hoa the next day and another survey trip had been made.

Not long afterwards, Gordon and Mr. Phuong went back with some Katu to the village of O-Rai perched on a high knoll in the foothills. The Katu fortify their villages by choosing almost inaccessible cliffs on which to build. This trip to O-Rai meant a practically perpendicular climb which taxed one's wind and muscles. Then the trail passed through some fields of pineapples growing on the side of the hill. When the top was reached, the view toward the east looked out to the sparkling South China Sea far in the distance and the jutting Marble Mountains on the seashore a few miles south of Da Nang. It was only a short way from the coastal highway, yet this land was a wilderness of wild mountains and these Katu, in their primitive huts, seemed centuries removed from civilization.

The tribespeople gave Gordon and Mr. Phuong a warm welcome and it was on this trip that one young man, named Trien, first heard the Gospel and later became one of our fine tribal workers. The next year, Trien entered our Bible School, as he could read and write Vietnamese, and spent one whole year with us. Two or three other Katu from his village also came to study the Word of God in Da Nang for several months.

Soon, kind friends in Los Angeles sent us their consecrated gift to build a house and chapel room for the Vietnamese evangelist and his family in this newly opened door of Phu Hoa. How could we carry on without these friends and their gifts from the homeland? The work began to get established. A number of Vietnamese tore down their Buddhist altars and pasted up mottos from the Word of God instead. One of their favorite texts is "Ton Vinh Duc Chua Troi" — "Praise God!" They also loved to have a picture from a Sunday school picture-roll sent by friends in America. From these, the Christians could instruct all who entered the house in the Way of Life, through Jesus Christ.

► 12 ◄

Les, the Hunter

THE HUNTER'S HORN WAS still sounding for our son Leslie and he was having a big share of tremendous excitement on his Big-Game expeditions. Viet Nam is one of the few virgin game-fields in the world today and Leslie had been in many sections, hunting every animal indigenous to the country — deer of different varieties, wild boar, tiger, leopard, gaur (wild black cattle), banteng (wild red cattle), elephant and wild buffalo.

Leslie took out high American government and military officials from Saigon and some British officers even came up from Singapore to go with him, and they got many trophies.

On his big hunting trips Les's outfit included around thirty elephants, with their drivers (mahouts), Mnong tribesmen, who were also skilled in tracking and skinning, building blinds in trees, (miradors) or bomas on the ground. They were pleased with their wages of seventy-five cents a day, with good feeding. He also had a Raday cook, called Ruih, who could make the meals for the white hunters and do their washing in the river. The tribesmen were all ready to work hard and go at any hour of the day or night.

Out from Banmethuot, which is one of the best hunting areas in the country, they would mount the elephants and jog off for a day or two into deep jungles. There they would make their camp, pitching tents, putting up hammocks or camp-cots, make rustic tables from bamboo, rustic benches and a fireplace of stones.

When Leslie came up to Da Nang to see us, he had some intensely thrilling stories to tell us of narrow escapes from dangerous wild animals, that would shake us to the marrow of our bones,

101

but we know that God was caring for him and had delivered him many times.

On one of these big game hunts, Leslie, with his helper, Ruih, and some trackers were out together one night with a headlamp, shooting wild boar for excellent tender meat for the hunters' larder in the jungle. They found a place where the ground was ploughed up by the hungry snouts of quite a drove of wild boar as they had been feeding on roots. The men followed their tracks and Leslie was able to shoot three boar.

Then he saw what he thought was another boar bounding through the tall grass toward him in the light of the headlamp. Leslie didn't have a good beam on him, but Ruih saw it was a tiger coming! He tried to yell but he had completely lost his voice from fear! The tiger, coming fast, was just on the last jump of 18 feet, with Leslie as his target, when Les saw the streak of yellow and black, the immense forepaws high in the air, claws out to strike. In a split-second, with cool daring, Les shot and the bullet hit the tiger in motion. With a terrible roar, the lord of the jungle fell dead — gaily painted in stripes, ruffled, fanged and bewhiskered — a beast of awful symmetry and power! Les' heart was pounding like a drum! Ruih and the trackers stood frozen in terror!

At last, Ruih pointed to a festering wound in the tiger's shoulder. "He's been hit here before!" he cried. Les later found out that this was probably a tiger that had gotten away from Mr. Ngo-Dinh-Nhu, the brother of the President of Viet Nam, who had been nearby on a hunt a few days previously. The tiger had been hiding there in the tall grass and Leslie and the others had come almost on top of him. A wounded tiger is the most dangerous of beasts!

He was around nine feet in length. The trackers bound the front feet, then the rear, thrust a pole between them and heaved his 350 pounds to their shoulders, and returned excitedly to camp. They would come back later for the wild boars Leslie had shot.

The tiger is the favorite trophy of the hunt in Viet Nam because of its glorious skin. The skinners with their knives swiftly peeled off the splendid robe of the tiger, a tedious job around the paws and ears — taking about six hours. Then they rolled it in salt and alum. Leslie had it sent into Banmethuot and on down to Saigon, by plane, to be well tanned. Later, we had the royal pelt on our living room floor at Da Nang for several months. Then Leslie sold it for a good price to some Americans returning to the homeland.

Tigers, the most gorgeous beasts in the world, are a great enemy of the tribespeople living in the jungles. Many children, playing at the edge of the fields while their parents are at work, are carried off. Or, as people go down to the village springs, tigers catch especially the old people, or any who have dropped behind the others on the lonely trail. They kill much livestock — goats, cattle, water-buffalo, pigs, horses. When they see the tiger dead, the tribespeople dance and prance about the fallen foe. He's not just a killer of livestock and people. To them, tigers are demons of the forest.

One of the most thrilling dinner-table stories Leslie told of his hunting adventures is of his encounter with a wild bull water-buffalo. This rare animal of the jungles and swamps of Viet Nam is one of the finest of all species of big game. Massively horned, it stands six feet tall, weighs close to a ton, is powerful and formidable.

Les says, "One day my party and I came upon a herd of these buffalo and gave chase. One bull came to bay, mighty, mean and big, and charged me. My hands raced to work the bolt of my 375 Magnum-Winchester and I shot some of the big bullets into the buffalo. Then I dodged behind a tree in time as the buffalo surged past me, his head lowered, sweeping his vast horns. He was so close that the froth from his spittle sprayed out onto my clothes. Skin prickling, heart racing, I poured more lead into the buffalo. He circled back again. His long, narrow head was thrust out, his eyes peering straight at me, his prodigious horns lying out flat. He was a ponderous creature but he was moving fast. I steadied for a sure shot and hit him in the head through the brain. He rolled over about at my feet. It had taken eight bullets to kill him. I had held four of these extra bullets between the fingers of my left hand in order to fit them quickly into the gun. (This is common practice among big game hunters.) I was reeling with exhaustion and intense strain! But, oh, boy! What a

Left: Little black honey-bea[r] Leslie picked up alongsid[e] road. Mother attacked [.] Later cub was given to S[a] Zoo, when he became too [dan]gerous to keep.

Below: Leslie and the wild water-buffalo he shot — most dangerous and bad-[tem]pered animal of the jungl[e]

Top: Les and wife
an American of-
ial from Saigon
ith leopard tro-
hy. Note tiger
aw hung from
ring around Les-
e's neck.

Below: Les and one
the Bantengs he
ot. They are wild
d cattle of the
pen forest.

trophy was that head with the great sweeping horns over six feet across — massive and impressive! I figure the wild water-buffalo is the most dangerous and bad-tempered animal of the jungle."

Leslie gave us one of the huge feet of this buffalo, nicely tanned, and we have it as a prize in Gordon's study. He sold the head as a splendid trophy to a hunter in Saigon.

We also have the tanned foot of one of the several bantengs Leslie has shot — the wild, red cattle of the open forests. A herd of these dashing through the green forest is a most beautiful sight — with their bright red-tan coats and curved horns. The banteng bull is a smaller imitation of his great black cousin, the gaur. The banteng is among the big-horned animals of the world.

Leslie and his hunter clients have come up to herds of gaur a number of times. They usually hunt these animals on elephant back as they are hard to stalk. They are the largest and noblest horned animal on earth, found only in North India, Malaya (where they are called "Seladang"), and Viet Nam.

The gaur stands between six and seven feet high at the humped shoulder. He is very ferocious and the herds slip like black ghosts through the vines and ten-foot high elephant grass of the deep jungles, where they like to feed. It takes skill and daring to bring one of these dangerous animals down. The head of the gaur gets the foremost place of honor in a trophy room. The curved yellow horns, tipped with black, are extremely heavy — at the base they are twenty inches in circumference.

Leslie sold one of the great mounted heads of a gaur that he shot, to an elite restaurant in Saigon, where it holds the prized place in the room today, over the central hearth.

One week, Leslie took out a young American, twenty years of age, who was in Saigon on a visit and wanted to go big game hunting. They saw a snake and the young man tried to grab it by the tail. Like a flash, Leslie shot the snake through the man's legs! It was a deadly banded-Krait. If the young fellow had grabbed it, he'd have been bitten and would have died soon after. So Leslie saved his life with his quick shot and then warned him never to pick up a snake in Viet Nam. All snakes must be regarded as poisonous and some are very deadly. They went on with the hunt and the young American shot a fine tiger from a tree-blind. He was very proud to have such a splendid trophy to take back to his home in America.

One day Leslie, himself, got bitten by a snake, just above the ankle. He was alone hunting near the side of the road. Able to crawl back to his jeep, he lay there helpless in a lonely jungle area. God delivered him by sending a young Frenchman who happened along in his jeep on this untraveled road. He found Leslie low, with a swollen leg and a high fever. He quickly drove Les the fifty miles into Banmethuot to the little hospital there, where he was treated many days for the snake bite venom. Leslie has a deep scar on his leg today from this terrible bite.

Another day, Leslie was traveling alone in his hunting jeep in a fairly well traveled section, when he saw by the side of the road a cute little black honey-bear cub, with a white chevron on his chest. He quickly jumped out of the car and grabbed the little bear. At that instant, a big mother bear rose up out of the brush not far away and came after Leslie with a heart-stopping roar! Like a good hunter, Les had his well-loaded rifle ready in his right hand. He speedily raised it to his hip with his one free hand and shot the bear just a few feet away from himself. If he hadn't been ready with his gun, the bear would have had him!

He waited there by the roadside until another car came along and the driver helped Leslie heave the big honey-bear up into Les' jeep. Leslie drove into the town of Banmethuot with the she-bear propped up beside him on the seat and the little bear scratching and clawing on his left arm, while he drove the jeep with his right hand. He was greeted by many cheers in the town.

Leslie kept the little bear as a pet until he got to be too old and dangerous. Then he gave him to the Saigon Zoo where he is today, well cared for.

Leslie has become quite well-known in South Viet Nam as a sportsman, with a good reputation, always much in demand. People were always after him for his stories.

But we were greatly relieved when Leslie left off this dangerous hunting for a time and took a job in American Aid, with their agricultural program among the Raday tribespeople.

▶ 13 ◀

Leprosy

IN 1950, GOD HELPED us to open up a Leprosarium at Banmethuot, among the Raday and Mnong tribes in South Viet Nam. Gordon had found the site, had the jungle forest cleared and put up cabins, some hospital buildings, a chapel and two homes for missionaries. Today this Leprosarium is being carried on very successfully by American nurses, an American doctor, and a number of Raday tribal nurses, treating around 250 in-patients and over 1000 out-patients under the Christian and Missionary Alliance. Eight years before we had claimed the establishing of this great project in Christ's name and faith had cried, "It shall be done!"

Now we were interested in exploring the leprosy situation in Central Viet Nam. No census had been taken and no one seemed to know the true facts.

On some of our trips up to Hue and our station out at Bang Lang for the Pakoh tribes, we heard that there were a number of leprosy patients in the Hue Hospital. So we hastened to visit them. There we found a group of more than 100 people with leprosy.

Their plight was appalling. They were all huddled together in a poor shack adjoining the hospital. They were like prisoners behind bars, living under filthy conditions — with no sanitation or hygiene. The air was poisoned with the stench of their putrifying flesh.

Some had faces covered with beady nodules and furrowed with deep wrinkles. There were those whose eyes were affected by leprosy and their sight was going. Some had no noses left and some had big, swollen "cauliflower" ears. Many had lost most of their fingers and toes, and there were open sores with no dress-ings, no bandages and the flies were thick. We wept as we moved among them and handed out Vietnamese tracts and gospels and prayed for them. Each time we visited them we brought them some bags of treats as well as what medication we had.

They were so happy to see us. Kindness and sympathy meant so much to them. They pleaded, "Can you help us?"

Our hearts were indeed moved to help relieve this awful distress.

We chose different sites at that time and one by one they would seem to be granted, but in the end they would be finally turned down by some office in Saigon as "being too good for lepers!" or "too dangerous because of the war."

We would need two centers. One place would be for the treatments, with the hospital, wards, living quarters for the patients, a school, a church. The other center would be for the Rehabilitation Program. Some patients would be healed of leprosy after two or more years of the good Sulphone drug treatment. But they would still be crippled by the effects of the disease. When they go joyfully to return home, they find they walk into a circle of stony faces which tell them clearly that they are no longer wanted.

They return sadly to us and we must have a Rehabilitation Center for them, where they will be made "whole." The stiff, claw hands have to be operated on, followed by hand exercises and massage by skilled nurses. Then the patients must be trained to use these hands in making things — gardening, carpentry, weaving, making toys and games like Chinese checkerboards and jigsaw puzzles. They could raise chickens in fenced-off pens; rear rabbits and pigs. In these ways, they could be prepared individually to go out and make a living in the outside world.

We had heard of a beautiful French summer resort on top of nearby Bana Mountain, 5,000 feet above sea-level, where before the Japanese and Viet Minh Communists wars, the French families of Da Nang spent their summers and week-ends. Although the road was impassable now, and the nearly 200 homes had been partially destroyed by the Viet Minh Communists, we had hopes that we could, some day, use this place as a missionary rest home.

We drove over what was left of a formerly good, paved road that wound and twisted up the steep mountain side through dense jungle. Woodcutters were busy hauling out firewood. Gordon

Above: Lepers living under filthy conditions at the hospital.
Left: Lepers listen to gospel records.
Below: Rehabilitation Center at Bana.

Some of the lepers who will find healing and new life at the Happy Haven Leprosarium.

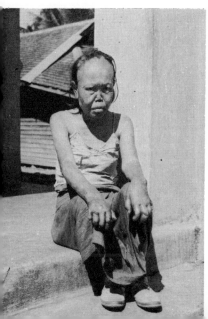

and some Vietnamese helpers walked the last eight kilometers beyond where the car could go. It was a rugged trip, crawling under thick bamboo, vines and creepers, over fallen logs, ever upward through the cool jungle forest. Finally on top, they revelled in the magnificent views on all sides. On the east was the city of Da Nang far below, and the South China Sea stretching out to the blue distance. On the north was the barrier range of mountains between Da Nang and Hue; and far out to the West was a vista of range after range of lavender-blue mountains.

The men found one of the French houses in fairly good condition and thought it would be well to fix it up some day as a missionary resort home. The whole mountain top was completely uninhabited. There was not a sign of life anywhere. It had been deserted like this since the Japanese war in 1941 — over fifteen long years. The trip down was quicker but they were pretty tired when they got back to the car.

At the foot of this Bana Mountain there is a beautiful park-like area with a stream flowing through it. It seemed to Gordon that this would be ideal for a leprosarium or a Rehabilitation site. The road into it from Da Nang was atrocious, as it also had been abandoned since the war and had not been fixed at all for the last fifteen years.

But Gordon kept visiting this area and spent days hacking his way through the masses of green, tangled, tropical growth, trying to get a glimpse of the terrain. It was hard to see more than a few feet into the dense jungle bush and as the place was very hilly, he had difficulty in finding suitable level spots that would be good for construction. Coming upon two beautiful cascades tumbling down from the heights above, through boulder-strewn gorges, he immediately envisioned free water power for a settlement here.

Gordon began the long drawn-out process of negotiating for a good tract of this land in these foothills of Bana. Starting with the local villagers he had a hard time convincing them that the lepers would not be dangerous. We received tentative authorization to cut roads through and clear sites for buildings at our own risk, pending final permission for the land.

At this time a fine Vietnamese Christian man and his wife, Mr.

and Mrs. Yen, offered to come up from Saigon to help us in this work. They were refugees from Hanoi and felt the call of God to work among the lepers.

Some of the leprosy patients at the Hue Hospital, who were responding well to the Sulphone drug treatment, offered to come and help clear off some of this Bana land. Mr. Yen would be in charge of them.

We built Mr. and Mrs. Yen a little bamboo house at the foot of the mountain, and Mrs. Yen was soon busy making a fine garden and raising chickens and pigeons. We put up a couple of houses, also, for the twenty leprosy patients who came to live out here and to start clearing some of the land. Mr. Yen had gospel services for them every night and twice on Sunday. Gordon and I also visited them frequently and before long they had all made their commitment to Christ.

A great new horizon was opening up before us — to bring life to these poor people with leprosy! We knew that the new medicine, the sulphone drugs, were really effective. These are a long-term treatment and bring good results in cases where the disease has not progressed too far. The terrible nodules will disappear and the spots will clear up. It is easy for children to get leprosy, but if we could get them early for treatment they could be cured.

What excitement for the people with leprosy! To have a new leprosarium opened for them! There they would receive cakes of soap, blankets, mats, clean living quarters. Kind nurses would be there to bind up their hideous, aching sores — evil-smelling and nauseating. They would have a good national evangelist to minister to them. They began to rejoice, saying, "Oh, I can be cured! I can be a human being again!"

One day we were out camping in one of our stations and our workers told us that there were some poor leper outcasts living down in a certain valley. We went down some steep hills and found them living in ragged, ugly little huts — off alone in their misery. Their faces were distorted and swollen, some noses were sunken in, legs were swollen and covered with sores, and fingers and toes were gone. They were dirty and had no clothing. Their hair was all tangled and wild. Their vocal cords had been eaten away and they could only whisper, "Help us! When can you take us to your leprosarium?"

One poor old leper kept coming the two miles every day to our campfire to see us. We could hear his breathing a long way off — like asthma rattles. His hair was long and matted, his lips all swollen and cracked, his face puffed and deeply furrowed. He was a man — but he looked just like an animal, and he cried, "Have mercy upon me!"

▶ 14 ◀

Phuoc Son, Center Number Nine

GORDON AND I REALIZED that our duty now, in the plan of God, was to return home to America to try to find some missionaries who would come out to help us in all these overwhelming tasks. In order to get the missionaries, we must join with some missionary society. As the people heard of the needs in Central Viet Nam they would eagerly share.

But before going home on furlough, we had another of the many pin-points (indicating possible strategic centers) on Gordon's wall-map to explore.

This was the village of Phuoc Son, the last Vietnamese outpost to another "uttermost" country. We would leave the coastal highway about half-way between Da Nang and Quang Ngai, and follow a trail, and then a river, into the fringe of a new tribal territory. Who would we find back in those wild jungle mountains that stretched on and on for one hundred miles, on to far-off Kontum and Dak To among the Sedang and Jeh tribes? Perhaps they would be the Katu or Cua tribespeople, as they were situated in between these two distinct tribal groups.

We took our Cua student, Quang, and our good Katu Christian, Trien, and two Vietnamese men student-preachers, Pham and Hoc, with us. We drove south down the coastal highway again, past the jade-green rice fields and Vietnamese farm hamlets. Then we turned west on to the side trail that would lead us in for about 25 miles to the river.

This was the rainy season and so we had to put chains on our wheels as the trail was full of deep ruts, gullies and slithering bogs. Holes two feet deep, full of water, would be directly in the path of the car. The sturdy Land Rover in 4-wheel drive, ploughed stubbornly through the mud, swinging to right and left — at times almost skidding into the black ooze of the rice fields bordering the edge of the road.

At the end of the trail we left the car in a Vietnamese village and took several sampans for our evangelistic party and baggage, going up a river for three hours. Each of the narrow river craft had two boatmen who stood up to row with long, heavy oars which they used with a peculiar sculling stroke. They had to battle skillfully with the many currents and boiling rapids. In places the water was so clear that the pebbles and sand appeared to be uncovered. Moss and ferns encrusted the banks and rocks with furry, lacy beauty. The river gurgled and sang with the currents and roared in the rapids.

By late afternoon we reached Phuoc Son, a humble village at the foot of heavily wooded mountains that rolled back, blue and purple against the sky. Most of the Vietnamese here had never seen white people before and they gazed at us open-eyed and open-mouthed.

We visited the village chief who was friendly and said we could camp in his little home. He told us that the Vietnamese government officials for this area had just called in the tribespeople from the mountains for a friendly political gathering and were giving them rice and salt. So we had arrived at a good time to see this tribe.

The people were gathered together in a big open shed, several hundred of them squatting on their haunches, silent, in groups around their baskets and smoky wood-fires. To us they were poorer and dirtier-looking than any of the other tribes we had ever seen — their coarse hair was long and matted, their naked bodies covered with grime. They wore just bits of ragged, filthy clothing and blankets. They had never seen a white person before but they didn't pay much attention to us. They seemed sullen and kept their heads down. This tribe had never submitted to the French and they had not yet submitted to the Vietnamese government.

Quang, our Cua tribesman, tried to talk to them but they didn't understand his Cua language. Then Trien tried to see if they

Wild tribespeople from behind Phuoc Son listening to the story of salvation for the first time.

Below: Christian congregation at Tra Bong — some Cua and some Vietnamese. Mr. and Mrs. Hap are at left.

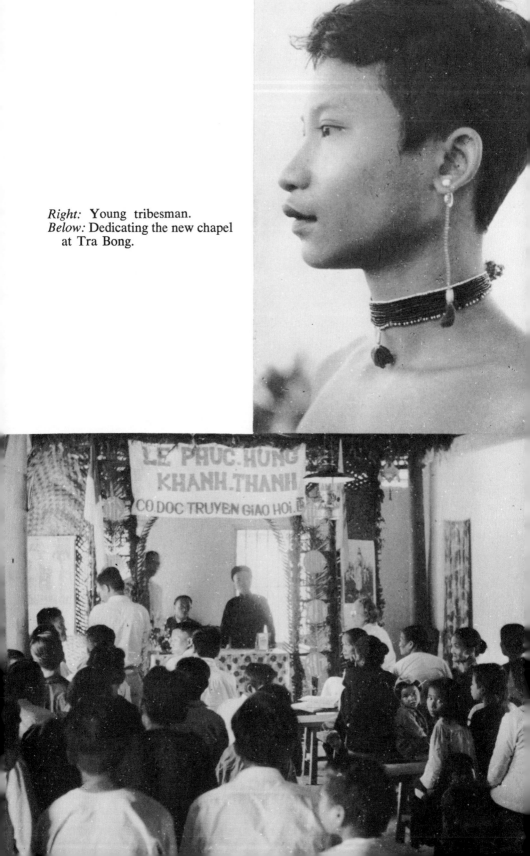

Right: Young tribesman.
Below: Dedicating the new chapel
at Tra Bong.

could understand his Katu language, but they shook their heads
and grunted that they didn't understand a word he said.

They had a different taste in beads. Many of them wore dog-
collar necklaces of red and black beads. There were no blue
beads like the Cuas favor, and there were no big black and white
beads, with tiger teeth, such as the neighboring Katu wear. A few
of their number could speak some Vietnamese and they said they
didn't build their houses up on stilts, like the Cua and Katu, but
down on the ground, in a long, undulating caterpillar fashion.
This was something new to us in tribal houses.

We set up our camp beds and mosquito-nettings in the Vietnamese chief's house, had a supper, and then hastened over to the
shed to try to preach to this big crowd of wild tribespeople. The
only name we could get from them was that they were the Lang
Ya people. This may be the name of their tribe or it might just
be the name of one of their villages. The Vietnamese simply called
them "Moi," meaning "barbarians."

One of their number could speak Vietnamese fairly well so we
got out our picture-rolls and flannelgraphs and in the light of
torch flares and our kerosene lantern, he interpreted for us from
Vietnamese into their tribal language. The shed was full of thick
smoke that choked us as we tried to tell them of God and His
Son, Jesus Christ, who loved them and died to save them and to
give them eternal life. It was all completely strange to them and
they listened with their heads down, still sullen, dull and cold.

The interpreter seemed bright enough and we taught him how
to bow his head and call on God in Jesus' name. It took him
quite awhile to learn how to say the name of Jesus Christ. They
had never heard this name before. We wondered how much of
the truth they grasped, and if they would remember Christ's
name.

Early next morning we hurried back to meet with the tribespeople again, but they had all gone away! Not one was left
in the camp or in the village! They must have taken off silently
in the middle of the night, as it was brilliant moonlight!

We were so sad and disappointed that we couldn't see more
of them! They were like a great herd of poor, pathetic lost
sheep. The enemy of souls has them in his dreadful power!

The Vietnamese officials told us that there were ten thousand of these tribespeople back in these mountains and they were very hard to reach. One had to go by river and then climb the steep mountains for days. One had to tread softly for there were many taboos where no government authority is yet established. But in a year or two the side road was to be pushed further west from Phuoc Son for another thirty miles where it would join with the main interior north-south highway running from Kontum, one hundred miles away, to Ben Giang and Thanh My, circling out to Da Nang. Then we would be able to reach these unknown tribal areas by car.

Our two bright, spiritual, young Vietnamese student-evangelists, Mr. Pham and Mr. Hoc, who were with us on this trip, volunteered to be the ones who would stay on here in Phuoc Son as pioneers to this tribe. The Vietnamese people, also, back in this remote section, had never yet heard the Gospel of Christ. So Pham and Hoc would begin to cultivate this Vietnamese field, too, as well as the tribes, and they would establish a good witness here.

Our evangelistic band spent the day visiting in the little huts of this village of Phuoc Son. A small plot of ground in front of each dark and mud cottage is beaten into a threshing floor for the rice grain, and it is hard and glaring in the sunlight. But in a corner of this good "platform" we usually find a shade tree and there we put up our flannelgraph board and picture-rolls and our audience crowds into the shady house and looks out upon the pictures, while we tell the stories of Jesus. We found the people very friendly.

We had a big meeting that night on the threshing-ground in front of the chief's cottage where we were camping. Pham and Hoc have good voices and so we had a lot of singing as this is a great attraction to the people and there is much Gospel in the songs. "Jesus Loves Me" and "I Am So Glad That My Father in Heaven" rang out over the little village. "We never hear any mention of love in our Buddhist religion," they cried. These songs became great favorites with the people.

We showed pictures, then each of the four students spoke; and Gordon gave a word. Then we drew in the net as always. Would anyone respond to the love of God by receiving the Lord Jesus Christ as their own personal Saviour? One old woman came forward, knelt and prayed. She was the first fruits of what, today, six years later, has become a fine little Christian community of thirty or more believers in Phuoc Son and another similar group of Christians in a nearby Vietnamese village with Pham still the pastor in charge.

Before we left the next day, to return to Da Nang by sampan and car, we were able to buy a little bamboo house there in Phuoc Son for Pham and Hoc where they could live and begin evangelizing.

► 15 ◄

The Worldwide
Evangelization Crusade

WE WERE FILLED WITH AWE at the way God had led and guided
us ever since we had returned to Viet Nam in February, 1956.
He had led us to launch out into a great, new work, among new
tribes of people. In less than two years, He had helped us to
open and establish ten new centers, organize a Bible School, and
make plans for a new Leprosarium in Central Viet Nam. We
were humbled before God. "To Him be the glory, great things
He hath done."

We had a good headquarters base in Da Nang, with two
houses, Bible School dormitories and a chapel. We were in the
center of new tribes of people in a district 400 miles in length.

Tra Bong, among the 30,000 Cua tribespeople, and thousands
of rural Vietnamese, now had a chapel, Vietnamese and Cua
evangelists, with some sixty committed believers.

Son Ha and Gi Liang, centers for 40,000 Hrey tribespeople, had
a Vietnamese evangelist and a Hrey student, Reo, preaching the
Gospel there. Money had already come in from faithful friends
in Los Angeles for the building of a chapel at Son Ha.

Bato, with around 40,000 more Hrey tribespeople, was opened,
with a chapel center and Vietnamese and Hrey evangelists.

Cam Phu, in the north, with 10,000 Baru tribespeople, was
opened with a chapelhouse for the Vietnamese evangelists there.

God had helped us open up Thanh My and Phu Hoa centers
among the 30,000 Katu. We had a fine Vietnamese student-
preacher and his wife, Mr. and Mrs. Cuu, in Thanh My now,

working with the nurse, Mrs. Thuan. A number of Vietnamese in this wild outpost, together with some Katu, had accepted the Lord.

For Phu Hoa, the other Katu center, twelve miles from Da Nang, we had already received another gift of money from our Los Angeles friends, to build a new chapelhouse for the pastor there. A good piece of land had been given us and there were some twenty Christians now in this section.

We had opened Bang Lang, six miles west of Hue and out from this market place were 13,000 Pakoh tribespeople back in the mountains. We had two Vietnamese student preachers there now.

Phuoc Son, in the heart of an unnamed tribe of 10,000 people, was now opened with two Vietnamese evangelists for this area.

We had had this steady succession of leading and opening before us and God had sent us, each month, all the money to support the Vietnamese and tribal workers in these centers and our Bible students in Da Nang — 50 workers in all — and the money to get land and houses built and some of the chapels up.

We had just stepped out at His command, taken His promises, believed them and His power had been made manifest and these miracles had happened. More than two hundred precious people had been won to God in these last two years. Christ was very real and precious to us.

There was great need to station white missionaries in each of these centers now. The tribal languages must be put into writing, learned and taught to the people, and the Word of God translated. These centers are wild frontier-posts with terrible jungles, steep mountains, rocky gorges with rushing, tumbling rivers. Everything is against the missionary in these frightening jungle countries that have defied the inroads of civilization successfully through the ages.

There were many more sections yet to be opened. The Jeh tribe of 20,000 people had never yet had a missionary or witness of any kind. There was the great Sedang tribe of 40,000 people with no missionaries. There were the 20,000 Bahnar tribespeople, and the 10,000 Bahnar-Cham; the 10,000 Rongao, and 30,000 Halang. We needed a strong mission board to adequately occupy these vast tribal and unreached Vietnamese areas with pioneer missionaries, linguists, nurses, doctors, equipment, buildings.

Seventy-five or eighty missionaries, in all, were needed to come to this Central part of Viet Nam as soon as possible. We had drawn up our plans for adequately occupying each of these tribal areas. Since we were the only ones who had ever made an intensive, thorough survey of these areas, we alone could speak with authority about them. We would not be satisfied with any feeble, slip-shod effort. It must be an all-out, speedy attack and occupation *now*.

Gordon had written to a number of mission boards in the States to see if they were interested in entering Viet Nam at this time. Several responded that they had been vitally interested in Viet Nam for many years. Gordon wrote an article in a leading Christian magazine entitled, "Viet-Nam, a Call for 150 Missionaries." As we had surveyed the situation we had seen the tremendous gaps needing to be filled.

Our committee of fine Vietnamese leaders was well able to carry on our work here on the field during our six-months' absence in America, provided we sent them the funds with which to carry on.

It was now October, and we thought we would like to spend Christmas with our son Douglas and his wife Ruth, and our grandchildren, Linda and Dougie, now in Marseilles, France. We would put on our Christmas program early, given by our Bible students in Da Nang — around December 16th — and then leave Da Nang on December 17th for Saigon and France.

But we didn't have one cent yet toward our fare! We thought we would like to buy return tickets as the round trip fare would save $355.00 on each ticket. So we asked the Lord for the money. This was a great deal of money indeed, but the expenditure was in the interests of these unreached tribes and Vietnamese and that was well worthwhile. We were not only asking for this sum of money, but we were asking God for a whole missionary society to oversee our work!

So we looked to God in simple faith. Simple faith links us up with a mighty God! It can defy all the hosts of hell. We stood on His promises all marked in our Bibles. We had had a little mustard-seed card in our Bibles for years, sent by friends. It had written on it the verse, "If ye have faith as a grain of mustard seed, nothing shall be impossible unto you." We held up our little mustard-seed to God every day. He also promised, "If thou canst believe, all things are possible to him that believeth." "Whatsoever things ye desire when ye pray, believe that ye *receive* them and ye shall have them." "Do not fear! Just believe! Do not stagger! Fear is unbelief." Praise Him, thank Him, worship and adore Him!

God answered these prayers as He laid it on the hearts of our wonderful friends in different denominations in the United States, Canada and England, and in a month's time we had all the money in for our tickets and travel needs, our tickets bought and our little Air France bags given us for the plane! Words simply failed us to express how thankful we were to God and our friends for all of these kind, sacrificial gifts for our trip!

Leslie met us at Saigon and the next day stood there, lonely, as our Super-G Constellation of Air France took us off. He would be all alone for Christmas and our hearts ached to be leaving him.

We were to make our "home" while on furlough with dear friends in Chicago, and when we entered their hallway we saw among the letters waiting for us on their hall table, a letter from Mr. Norman Grubb, director of the Worldwide Evangelization Crusade. He had read Gordon's recent article on "Viet Nam, a Call for 150 Missionaries" and he asked permission to reprint it in the W.E.C. Magazine, "World-Wide."

Gordon immediately phoned Dr. Grubb at the W.E.C. headquarters, Fort Washington, Pennsylvania, a suburb of Philadelphia, and said that if Dr. Grubb was interested in Viet Nam, Gordon would get on a bus the next day, meet him in Fort Washington and talk things over with him.

We had read the books on the great life of C. T. Studd, written by Dr. Norman Grubb, telling of the wealthy, brilliant cricketer of Oxford who gave up all his riches and fame to go out and live in a little hut in the wilds of the heart of Africa, and who had founded the Worldwide Evangelization Crusade. Was this the mission God was leading to enter with us into Viet Nam? The very next day, Gordon was on the Greyhound bus going to Philadelphia, with Stanley, Ginny and me seeing him off at the Chicago bus depot.

Gordon was favorably impressed with the W.E.C. setup at their beautiful headquarters on Camp Hill in Fort Washington. The main building is a stately, hundred-year-old mansion house, Tudor design, of square gray stone, thick walls, towers, dormers, turrets and tall chimneys. We have the same doctrinal beliefs as W.E.C. They have a leprosy and medical program and they were interested in our new Leprosarium project in Central Viet Nam.

For years the W.E.C. Mission had been interested in entering Viet Nam and in Dr. Grubb's book on C. T. Studd, which he had written some years previously, he says, "God will surely give W.E.C. entry to the land of Indo-China (now called Viet Nam) as He has to seventeen other countries."

Was God now answering this prayer-goal of years in the W.E.C. circles?

Dr. Grubb asked Gordon to think the matter over of joining the W.E.C. In three months' time, on April 1st, they would be holding their quarterly staff meeting at Fort Washington and by that time, perhaps, we would all know the definite leading of God. We were hoping to return to Viet Nam in May when our Bible School would be closing and there would be twenty-six new student-evangelists to place in new tribal areas.

After much prayer and consultation with a number of missionary societies during those two and a half months, the Lord led us to return to Fort Washington, Pennsylvania, into the fellowship of the great faith missionary crusade — W.E.C. We knew we could have had good fellowship if we had joined other groups, but it seemed to us that the door into W.E.C. opened the widest and the quickest in the short time we had there in America.

On April 1, 1958, we were given a warm reception as we met with the quarterly staff meeting of W.E.C. at Fort Washington. Their acceptance of us was unanimous. We were able to cable our staff of fifty Vietnamese and tribes colleagues on the field that our mission, "Operation Service," which we had organized two years previously, had now become a part of the Worldwide

Evangelization Crusade. This meant that W.E.C. was now in Viet Nam.

There was much rejoicing in the W.E.C. staff that the Lord had now opened this door into Viet Nam and we praised God for answered prayer for us, too, by leading us into W.E.C.

The temporary name, "Operation Service," was now dropped and W.E.C. would be our English name in Viet Nam. Our Vietnamese name is always the Co Doc Truyen Giao Hoi, meaning "Society for the Propagation of Christianity."

The Worldwide Evangelization Crusade has a ministry in many lands with 750 crusader missionaries following, under God, the footsteps of its great founder, C. T. Studd. It is strictly a faith mission looking to God to move upon the hearts of His people to supply the needs of the work. All gifts for our field would be sent to the W.E.C. headquarters and would be forwarded to us without any deductions whatever. We felt deeply honored to belong now to this great Crusade.

All W.E.C. candidates must spend six months, at least, at a W.E.C. headquarters after their missionary training, where the principles of this Crusade are learned.

Our Stanley and Ginny visited the W.E.C. headquarters at Fort Washington in April and began to seek the Lord's will regarding making application for missionary service in Viet Nam under the W.E.C. After finishing their special missionary course at Moody Bible Institute in June, they would enter Fort Washington headquarters as candidates.

In May, when it was just about time for Gordon and me to return to Viet Nam, we received a startling cable from Leslie in Saigon, saying that the doctors there feared he had Hodgkin's Disease and he must return to America immediately! This terrible disease is incurable cancer of the blood, life-expectancy is usually short and there is no human remedy, so far, for it. Our hearts were indeed crushed with the blow! We sent out a call to all of our prayer-warriors for much prayer for Leslie, and the W.E.C. friends stood with us in faith that God would do a miraculous work in his heart, life and body. In the name of our Lord Jesus Christ, we rebuked this awful disease and we looked to God to heal Leslie. As we trusted in Him, He gave peace.

WAGGONER CHRISTIAN CHURCH

Through the kindness of Dr. Lewis Robbins of Washington, D.C., Co-Ordinator for Cancer Control in the U.S.A. (who had been out in Viet Nam and helped us to obtain a lot of equipment from American Aid for our first Leprosarium at Bamenthuot in 1951 to '53), Leslie was invited to enter the National Cancer Institute at Bethesda, Maryland, for free treatment. He would get the best diagnosis here of any research hospital in all the U.S.A.

Gordon had to return to the field in May to look after the work, but I stayed on in America to meet Leslie when he would arrive. Dr. and Mrs. Robbins graciously invited me to stay at their home in Washington while Leslie would enter the Bethesda Hospital.

Leslie flew from Viet Nam where he had been working with American Aid and also doing some more big game hunting on the side, and on his way through France, he stopped in Paris. Gordon was able to meet him there and Douglas, Ruth and children came up from Marseilles and also visited with Leslie and their dad again.

When Leslie arrived by plane in Washington, he looked better than we expected, but he had lumps on his neck. We took him immediately to the National Cancer Institute at Bethesda, Maryland, and five or six doctors there began a careful examination of him. He was in the hospital for more than a month and the time of diagnosis was a great strain for us but the Lord was near.

Leslie, himself, was in good spirits and the patients near his room, and all the doctors and nurses who cared for him there in the hospital, were delighted to hear his hunting stories and to see his many photos of his big game hunts in Viet Nam.

Then came the wonderful day when the doctors pronounced that they found no trace at all of Hodgkin's Disease in Leslie! The Pasteur Institute tests in Saigon and from Paris had both said that he had the disease! But either they had made a mistake or God had wonderfully delivered Leslie! We immediately wired Gordon in Viet Nam the great news of victory, and we were all rejoicing.

Later on, after Leslie left the Research Institute, he had a severe attack of pain and it was found that his pancreas was infected. He had to go on a strict diet for awhile but was soon perfectly well. God was so merciful! How could we praise and thank Him enough!

As the Air France Super-G landed at the Saigon airport, there was Gordon to meet me. What joy and peace to be together again! We are as one in purpose as the two wings of a bird.

Saigon in December was pleasantly warm and it was nice to hear the pretty sing-song Vietnamese speech again.

Next day we flew up to Da Nang and home. It was a delight to be back, for we love our work. Many of our native workers and the new Bible School class who had entered in September, 1958, were there to meet me. We had three days of joyous conference together. They loved to hear all about their friends in America and Britain.

► 16 ◄

Seven New Stations

AFTER GORDON HAD RETURNED to Viet Nam in May, alone, God had helped him to make swift advance into seven new tribal areas never before entered with the Gospel. What used to be just marks on the map, prayed over and studied for months and years, now became new missionary outposts.

When Bible School closed in May, there had been twenty new, bright young men students who were capable now of manning these stations and Gordon and Mr. Nhut placed the best of them in the seven new centers. The rest of them went to help out on the already established nine mission stations.

A wonderful new house-trailer had arrived for us, a gift from kind, generous friends in America, and Gordon took off by Land Rover, hauling this trailer on all his new trips. It is 12 feet long, built strongly, like a truck, especially made for our terrible roads. It has shock absorbers on the wheels and on the hitch which hold the trailer steady on the rough places. Gordon enjoyed sleeping in one of its comfortable beds and spent many nights camping in it along the road. Anh Hai was with him to make his meals on the smart little Butane-gas stove. It was just like living in America! Gordon was able to take different students along with him. These would be stationed in the new centers.

He drove hundreds of miles into these seven strategic places. He secured permission from the government authorities, bought land, rented or purchased a small native shack and placed a worker and his family there.

Of course, all of this required funds, and God was supplying this need in a marvelous way. At this time, word was received from the Association for Native Evangelism of Tulsa, Oklahoma, offering to support as many pioneer national workers in new areas as we could give them. There were absolutely no strings attached to this wonderful offer. We would be required to send monthly reports from each worker, and the support would be on a temporary basis, to help the infant churches become self-supporting after a few years. We eagerly responded to this magnificent offer and from that time on, this great organization has made it possible for us to make a steady advance into absolutely unreached areas. Without such sacrificial gifts from the homelands there can be little advance and little work accomplished. We are always happy to receive gifts from God's praying people, "rich in faith," no matter what their denomination may be.

Gordon first drove fifty miles south of Da Nang on the coastal highway to a town called Tam Ky. Turning west from there down a rough side road, he went into a place twenty miles away at trail's end, called Bong Mieu, a Vietnamese farming community, with the Cua tribespeople living in the surrounding wooded hills and mountains. Gordon bought a little house and placed one of our brightest young students, Cang, and his wife here. Cang's wife, a brilliant student, had led the whole Bible School during the last year. This was a hard, lonely place for this attractive young couple but God was going to bless and use them mightily in this area.

Gordon next drove on farther south, turning off just before reaching Quang Ngai, down the Son-Ha side road. He opened up a heavily populated Vietnamese market town, fifteen miles before reaching the Hrey center of Son Ha. This place is called Dong Ke. Some Hrey tribespeople also come into this center and there were thousands of rural Vietnamese people here who had never heard of Jesus Christ. Gordon was able to get government permission and rent a hut here for our student preacher, Mr. Thanh, and his wife and family. God had a great work for them to do in this area.

Then Gordon and his party drove back to the coastal highway again and went on south, past Quang Ngai to the side road leading through to Bato. Passing Bato, they drove on down the beautiful Hrey river valley to Gia Vuc, another densely populated section

Top: Swaying, rocking trailer follows Land Rover over treacherous, dangerous roads.
Below: Chapel at Kim Son, in the heart of communist country.

Left: Pastor Giang, his wife and four little girls, and friends in front of new chapel at Ankhe.
Right: Vietnamese children at Ankhe.
Below: Mr. and Mrs. Dich in front of their mission house at An Lao.

for the Hrey tribe. He put one of our students and his wife in a Hrey longhouse there.

Then he went back to the coastal highway again and drove on farther south to another center for the Hrey tribe, twenty miles west, off the highway to a place called An Lao. It is a big Vietnamese market center with thousands of unreached Vietnamese people all along the way, as well as the countless tribal villages back in the wild mountains behind An Lao. An interior road will some day be completed that will link up these Hrey tribespeople behind An Lao with those of Bato, Gia Vuc and on to Son Ha, Gi Liang and Dong Ke. Gordon placed a worker and his wife, Mr. and Mrs. Dich, in An Lao, renting a small bamboo home for them.

After An Lao, he pushed farther south to a village at the end of a beautiful trail, called Kim Son. This is the frontier marketplace for the wild Bahnar tribespeople, living by the thousands back in the mountains behind Kim Son. He rented a little place here for Mr. Thai and his wife.

Gordon next traveled on as far as the big city of Qui Nhon on the coast, which is 250 miles south of our city of Da Nang. Near there, he took a road branching west into the mountains for sixty miles to the center of Ankhe among the Bahnar tribe. Here he rented a house and placed a fine worker and his wife and children, Mr. and Mrs. Giang, in this great area. Some day a road through the mountains will link Ankhe directly with Kim Son.

Gordon then returned to Qui Nhon and drove on farther south, then went in on a trail west to Phuoc Lanh among the Bahnar-Cham tribespeople. He rented a little house here and put in one of our finest evangelists and his wife and children, Mr. and Mrs. Vui.

At this time God wonderfully answered prayer and sent us two generous gifts to meet our needs. Each was a gift in memory of a loved one who had been interested in missionary work and who had just recently passed away. One gift of $5,000.00 was sufficient to pay for our headquarter's house which included the 15 outside rooms and bathing and toilet facilities for our Bible School students. The other gift of $2,700.00 purchased the other house that we were using then for the Bible School building as classrooms, dining room, kitchen and chapel.

Later, when more money came in, we were able to build a large classroom chapel at the back of our property and turn this house into a residence for our new missionaries.

We were also able to buy the third house on our compound and soon had it ready for the coming of more missionaries. They would all have to stay in Da Nang for about two years as they studied the Vietnamese language before going on out to occupy Mission centers.

Our hearts truly welled up in praise to God for all these manifestations of His grace.

▶ 17 ◀

Jungle Beach-heads

Soon after Easter, the Cornells, Dave and Gwen, who were visiting us from W.E.C. Headquarters, Anh Hai, Gordon and I, left Da Nang for a visit to Phuoc Son. We drove the 45-mile trip over the bumpy roads, thick with dust in this season, to where we changed to three sampans for the trip up the river to Phuoc Son. A Vietnamese mother and son manned the boat Gwen and I were in. They stood poised on each end of the craft, silhouetted against the bright blue sky and puffy, white clouds. The handsome youth was picturesque, wearing a cone-shaped, palm-leaf Vietnamese hat with a blue ribbon under his chin. He sang a hauntingly weird native chant as he sculled us along in rhythmic measure.

The river took us deeper into the primitive mountain hinterland country and at times our rowers had to get out and push the boats up the swift, shallow stream. Dave jumped out frequently to get good shots on his movie camera.

We arrived at Phuoc Son late in the afternoon and our two Vietnamese evangelists, Hoc and Tin, were down at the river to meet us, beaming with delight. At that time, Pham, who had opened the work here with Hoc over a year previously, was away doing his military service. After two years in the army, he was able to return to our Bible School and is now stationed at this post again.

We walked up a path for one-half mile to their little new chapel-house. It was just one room made of bamboo and thatch. Sections of the wall could be raised to let in the breezes. The big open door framed a picture-view of the village huts backed with blue-massed mountains.

We soon fixed our sleeping cots in the room, tied up our mosquito nets and made little screened-off "dressing rooms" for ourselves. Our supper was prepared in the tiny cook-shed at the back. The fire was of wood and the smoke burnt our eyes.

Forty Christians and many others of the village crowded to the house for the evening meeting. We hung up our bright gasoline lantern and the people sat on rows of benches outside the house, and we had a good meeting.

The night was shot with patterns of sparks from myriads of fireflies. Trees, bushes and grass were ablaze with their eerie, wavering light. Overhead the brilliant stars studded the dark sky and the twinkling fireflies dotted the black trees. At a glance it was impossible to see where the star-lit sky ended and the insect-lit vegetation began. Frogs and crickets made the night pleasantly vocal.

The next morning Gordon and Dave Cornell, with Hoc and Anh Hai, went off on a ten-mile trek up to two of the nearest villages in the wild tribal mountain country.

Gwen and I stayed with Tin in Phuoc Son village. While the men were gone for three days, we visited among the native huts every morning and afternoon. One old deaf man received Christ and we were able to encourage and cheer many of the Christians in their little houses. We had well-attended meetings each night.

At noon, on our fourth day in the village, Gordon and Dave returned, looking like very tired pioneer crusaders after their trek of ten miles down the mountains since early morning. Gordon had a bright red, velvety, jungle flower stuck gaily in his sport shirt and Dave had let his beard grow and was leaning on his staff.

The people back in these mountains are quite primitive. Gordon still couldn't find the proper name for them. They say, "We don't have a name." One of the first of these tribesmen that Gordon had met on his first visit, said he was a "Lang Ya," so we are still calling them by that name until we can learn better. The tribespeople didn't know the names of the surrounding Katu and Cua tribes, so this showed that they do not travel much.

For an hour the men had hiked through rolling grasslands,

then entered thick jungles where the blood-suckers clung to them
every few feet and tormented them. Their path took them
through black, muddy pools, then clear running streams, crossing a dozen times in knee-deep water. Then they began to climb.
They met some Vietnamese soldiers and some tribesmen cutting
the brush from the trail and the chief accompanied them back
to his village. During a pause, he found Gordon's walking pole
was rough on the hands, so he kindly smoothed it off with his
hatchet. These Lang Ya were only now being civilized. Until a
year or so previously, they were independent and hostile, and they
are still unstable, so the government was keeping soldiers in each
village.

With pounding hearts the men climbed up and down, passing
many dangerous hidden traps for catching wild boar and deer.
Then they finally came to the village of Nuoc Moc — the first
time a white missionary, perhaps the first time any white man
had ever entered here. Our Vietnamese evangelists had made
several visits there so the people were not too surprised to see them.

It was the strangest tribal village Gordon had ever seen! It
consisted of only one very long house, low on the ground, cling-
ing to the jungle slope, undulating with the rolling hill like a great
caterpillar. Twelve families lived in it, and tiny openings led
into their small, dim apartments. Smoke seeped out through the
thatched roof.

Inside, it was impossible for the white men to stand up as the
ceiling came down to shoulder height, and only here and there
could Gordon find an opening through which he could put his
head and stand up straight. A dozen rattan hammocks hung
from the house-poles, while over each mud fireplace hung a
square frame for drying tobacco leaves, corn and meat.

Gordon and Dave threw down their bags and unrolled their
bedding on mats the chief provided. They were squeezed between
the mud fireplace and the wall, which was covered with the
sacred remains of their sacrifices — buffalo skulls, wild pig and
dozens of monkey skulls and tufts of deer's tail. These were all
taboo to touch. The chief was giving the men the place of
honor, but he warned them not to touch any of those things
sacrificed to the spirits. Some of the meat bones were terribly

smelly, so Gordon and Dave asked the chief if he would kindly put them farther away.

At night, the Vietnamese soldiers in the village told all the men to go and listen to the evangelists preach, so twenty-one half-naked tribesmen came and sat around their candlelight. Women and children peered through the smoky gloom and hid when the missionaries looked their way. Gordon and Dave couldn't make friends with the children at all, as they were desperately afraid of the white men.

Next morning, they walked for two hours to the next village, Tra No. The tribespeople there were surly and rude. When the men gathered them together in the evening after they had returned from their rice fields, to hear about Christ, the tribesmen frequently interrupted the white men, saying, "Stop! We don't want to hear about that." "Don't be silly, no one ever rose from the dead!" When Hoc, the Vietnamese preacher, told them to give attention because he was going to ask them questions afterward, they shouted "Stop! We'll never remember! Don't tell us any more!"

The missionaries wondered what kind of a reception they would have had if there had not been soldiers in the vicinity. Truly these were among the most primitive people one could find. They were filthy, choking with tuberculosis, ignorant and — lost! If we did not seek them out and champion their cause, who would? We felt burdened over these awful facts! This is the latter half of the Twentieth Century, when nations are reaching for the moon and possibly Venus — but here were poor, unreached tribal people with their gongs and drums reverberating out over these hills and their diabolical screams piercing the night as their sacrifices were made to the demons.

In May, Mr. Alfred Ruscoe also came from W.E.C., Fort Washington, Pennsylvania, to spend several weeks with us.

He was with us when the hot weather was at its height and the humidity at times was suffocating. Some days not a current of air circulated and the tropical heat weighed heavily upon us. But in these months of May, June, and July our town of Da Nang is full of the scarlet bloom of the Flame of the Forest trees, blazing red against the dark blue mountains. The ocean, too, is of un-

Above: Vietnamese military jeep has just turned over on road from Gia Vuc.

Below: Mr. and Mrs. Dave Cornell take a ride on elephant belonging to Yong, Christian Baru tribesman near Cam Phu.

Top: Part of the "Caterpillar" longhouse of the wild tribespeople behind Phuoc Son. The missionaries could not stand upright in it.
Below: The people in this Tra No village longhouse "were surly . . ."

Top: Mr. and Mrs. Dave Cornell and the author camped at this Thanh My chapel on the edge of the Katu jungle.
Below: Mr. Yong's elephant bows before Mr. Kinh.

earthly beauty, warm, calm and blue. On the beach there is only the faint whisper and gurgle of the water as it laps on the sand. We took our guests for some wonderful swimming and picnics by the sea whenever we had a few days in Da Nang.

Mr. Ruscoe arrived just in time for the closing exercises of our third year of Bible School. Dave Cornell took movies of the students in their closing day of school — twenty-four young men and women, in single file, with measured step, coming slowly across the compound to the music of "The Heavens Are Telling" from Haydn's "The Creation," played on my little pump organ. Each wore a small bow of ribbon, red for the girls, navy blue for the boys (their own idea), and they were all dressed in white, the girls in their long, slim, silk tunics over white trousers, and the men in Western clothes. They marched up the aisle of their classroom and took their appointed seats in perfect order.

Up at the front of the room the students had drawn on a large blue silk background the W.E.C. emblem of the Cross against the World, with the Bible and a sword, and the name, "Worldwide Evangelization Crusade."

The students had special song numbers for the closing exercises, and Mr. Ruscoe and Dave Cornell gave messages, translated by Mr. Nhut into Vietnamese.

Then we had a full week of conference together with the students and our thirty-five Vietnamese workers and their wives. There were daily meetings of the whole group from the 6 A.M. prayer meetings to the nightly meetings. The Conference was a delight of spiritual blessing to all of our people.

Our Mission Statutes and Constitution were all discussed by the Committee with the W.E.C. leaders from America. This was given legal recognition and approval by the government of Viet Nam.

Our visitors wanted to see as many of our stations as possible and so we were almost constantly on the go all the time they were with us.

After the Conference, we all drove out to our station at Bong Mieu where God had been wonderfully blessing our young workers, Mr. and Mrs. Cang. Over one hundred Vietnamese and Cua tribespeople had accepted Christ in Bong Mieu and in another station nearby, An Trung, that the Cangs had opened to the Gospel. On this trip we saw forty of these new believers baptized.

Then we took the long trek south and west into the mountains to Ankhe. We spent several days there with Mr. and Mrs. Giang and the Christians and had a blessed baptismal service for twenty-five of the believers.

We next visited the Cham-Bahnar tribes at Phuoc Lanh, nearly 250 miles south of Da Nang where our Vietnamese evangelists, Mr. and Mrs. Vui and their children, were working. Thousands of people from this tribe had been brought out of the mountains to resettle in safety here from the Communists, who were continuing to infiltrate all the mountain areas more and more. Already the Roman Catholics saw this great opportunity to reach these tribespeople and they were taking over whole villages of these resettled people. Vui was working night and day visiting the tribal villages and the needy back-country Vietnamese people, none of whom had ever heard one word of the Gospel before.

On the way back, as we passed the city of Qui Nhon, Mr. Ruscoe left us, taking the plane there back to Saigon and on to other places on his world W.E.C. Mission tour.

Our son, Leslie, arrived out in Viet Nam again at this time, in excellent health and ready to work in the American Government Aid program.

He went with the Cornells and us on our next trip, to Bato. Gwen and I stayed in this station while Mr. Lich, Dave, Gordon and Leslie went on to open new stations in the Province of Kontum. They followed a new, strategic road just being made by American Engineers, from Gia Vuc, zig-zagging up 2,600 feet into new tribal country.

They followed just behind the bulldozers on the wide dirt road with many unfinished places, which only a car with four-wheel drive could negotiate. Several steep elbow-turns obliged them to back up and edge their way around the curves, then up 30 per cent grades as the road switch-backed up to the top. They often had to get out and walk, for the grades were steep and slippery. They had to hold the car from tipping over on its side in some places and they crawled over piles of rock that had been blasted out of the mountains.

It was a frightening ordeal at times, especially when on their way down one steep incline, a Vietnamese military jeep slid around a curve too fast and turned over in front of them. No one was hurt, but they were on the edge of a terrible precipice. This can all be seen today in the film, "Jungle Beach-heads."

The men pushed on to Kontum. No Protestant missionary had ever preached in this great interior province, inhabited by 87,000 tribespeople and nearly as many Vietnamese. One hundred years ago, some Roman Catholic French priests fled the persecution on the coast and settled in Kontum, building up a strong work in and around the city.

Gordon received authorization for our mission to preach in this province. He rented a small house at Kontum and soon put three Vietnamese preachers here in this district. One was our experienced worker and his wife, Mr. and Mrs. Kinh, who had opened Cam Phu in the north, but who would now head this important new work in this province, manning the work in Kontum. The other two workers were put in at Dak Sut and Plateau G.I. In the Dak Sut area there are scores of Sedang, Jeh and Halang tribal villages. Dak Pek, Dak Ro-Tah and Dak Gle are big Jeh areas that would be opened soon. Dak To is the important center for 40,000 Sedang tribespeople. At Plateau G.I. are 4,000 Mnom tribespeople. It would be the first time in history that these tribes would be contacted with the evangelistic message.

The workers also soon found a sympathetic re-settlement Vietnamese village, 25 miles out of Kontum, called Dak Psi. They began evangelizing there and 33 Vietnamese quickly professed conversion. Many people were coming into these three new stations to inquire about the Lord. The chief medical officer at Kontum gave the workers a supply of good medicines for the needy in their districts. So we had a fine reception in the Kontum Province and the work there was off to a good start.

While the men were away for ten days on this Kontum trip, Gwen Cornell and I had a good ministry at Bato. Mr. Lich had made two tiny "guest-rooms" in the white-washed, thatched-roof chapel there and we were very happy to have these nice little quarters for our camping.

How we revelled in the beautiful scenery of the mountains and river valley of Bato. In the fresh, early morning as we ate our breakfast, we'd watch the violet mountain peaks of the great range in front of the chapel slowly emerging from a sea of clouds illumined by the long rays of the rising sun from across the valley.

Each morning and afternoon, our little "Band," including Mrs. Lich, An ("Grace"), the nurse, daughter of Mr. and Mrs. Nhut, who was helping now in Bato, and several other Vietnamese Christian men and women, with Gwen and me, went visiting in the Bato Vietnamese village and also over the rice field narrow dikes to many tribal villages. We usually entered some friendly hut where many people would soon gather. We preached the Word with the help of our pictures and illustrated song sheets and answered many of their questions. It was hot around noon, walking in the blazing May sun, and twice Gwen and I became sick from the great heat and fatigue. But God gave much blessing and we were able to help a number of precious souls find the Saviour.

One morning, a Vietnamese man who was dying of tuberculosis called us to come to his hut. Mr. Lich had been dealing with him in the past weeks about his soul, and now he was ready to believe. After our messages, he and his wife, two little sons and two neighbors all prayed. Just two days later, the man with tuberculosis died peacefully in Christ.

The next place we visited was Thanh My, camping in our chapel there. The second night after our arrival, a tiger stole into the Katu village of Mo-O, across the river from Thanh My, and dragged off a water buffalo. That same night the heat was so stifling that Gwen and Dave had pulled their cots outside and slept under the stars. But had they known that a tiger was prowling around so near they would not have taken such a risk.

We always enjoyed the early mornings, exquisitely fresh, with the mists like white tulle on the mountains, myriads of birds singing, gibbon apes calling boldly from the mountain forests, and monkeys playing in the great trees across the river from us, making the branches flop and balance after their bounds.

But the Communists were infiltrating badly now into this interior country. The day we arrived at Thanh My, the local administrator called into our chapel to warn us of the danger back in the mountains. This area was now heavily patrolled by Vietnamese soldiers. All night long the woods and hillsides resounded with shouts from these soldiers on duty, answering the periodical roll-call. They kept waking us from our sleep but it was comforting to know they were there on guard.

The Katu villages far back in the mountains have always been hostile to the government. The Communists now were seeking by threats and trickery to turn the people more than ever against the authorities. So these unfriendly Katu set out lance-traps along the trail for the Vietnamese. While we were at Thanh My a Vietnamese man stepped on the trigger of one of these hidden traps and a spear whizzed through his hip, coming out at the groin. With the help of another man he managed to get to our station where our nurse, Mrs. Thuan, dressed his wound. Fortunately, the lance had not been poisoned.

Each night our little bamboo chapel was packed, and there were more faces outside peering through the windows.

One little man, a helper to Mrs. Thuan, called Bon, was so deeply moved when we showed him a picture of the Crucifixion, through a Story-graph Viewer, that he refused food for several meals and wept, saying over and over, "I don't know why He should have suffered like that for me!" The Message of Calvary was very real to him. Of this world's goods he had nothing — just a rag or two for clothing. But he had found Christ, the Saviour, so he had eternal riches that are far greater than all this world's gold. Dave gave him one of his own shirts, and he gazed into Dave's eyes — his whole soul saying, "Thank you!"

When at the end of four days, we said good-by to our friends at Thanh My, there stood Bon with the tears streaming down his face. Clasping Dave's hand in his, he pointed with the other hand to the heavens. He was saying, "If we never meet again upon this earth, we'll all meet up there." Bon, today, is still serving the Lord as a faithful helper to the nurse, Mrs. Thuan.

We next visited Cam Phu, the most northern station. The Cornells enjoyed the scenery here, enchanting cone-shaped, turreted-castle rocky mountains pointing up everywhere. We camped in our bamboo meeting-place built two years previously. Mr. Phan

WAGGONER CHRISTIAN CHURCH

and his wife had replaced Mr. and Mrs. Kinh here and they are devoted workers for God.

We visited the village of Yong — one of our Christian Baru tribesmen. His elephant took the Cornells for a ride, thrilling them, as the grave old giant, the color of mud, paraded them around the village on soundless pads. He flapped his big pink ears and stretched his long trunk along a veranda which was up on stilts, into the door of a house to steal sweet potatoes out of a basket.

We also visited the village of Oai, another Baru Christian. We followed a foot-trail in for a mile or so from the main road, going through tall, thick grass that can cut like a razor. Oai had attended our Bible School at Da Nang for a few months, then grew so homesick that he had to return to his village.

As we arrived in Oai's village we watched the women pounding their rice with tall wooden pestles in rhythmic blows upon the paddy in the bottom of their wooden mortars. The tribeswomen everywhere are always busy — cutting wood, drawing water or pounding the rice. We called to all the people to come to see our pictures and hear our message and a good crowd of them climbed up the ladder with us into Oai's hut, perched high on wooden posts. Oai translated for us into Baru as we spoke Vietnamese.

We were able to visit at least fifteen of our stations with the Cornells, spending from several days to a week in each place. Our hearts were truly uplifted by the visits of these sympathetic W.E.C. leaders. We would have loved to have kept them in Viet Nam as they would make excellent missionaries, but they had to return to the home base in America where Dave Cornell is now the Foreign Secretary for the North American W.E.C.

Some new Crusaders were now arriving on the field and this was a great comfort to us. Miss Joan Burridge, a nurse from England, and Miss Joyce Hedwall, from the United States, arrived in June and were soon hard at work in the language study.

Dr. and Mrs. Billman, after nine years in leprosy work in W.E.C. in Africa, arrived with their four children in July, bringing with them their experience and deep insight into the things of God.

Miss Mary Henderson, a secretary to help Gordon with all his heavy bookkeeping and correspondence, arrived from the Bible College of Wales, where she had spent 23 years on the staff and had been secretary to that great prayer-warrior, Rees Howells. With her was Miss Daphne Lydamore from England, a former school teacher. Oliver Trebilco arrived from Australia.

After a few more months we would be welcoming our own children, Stanley and Ginny; and Roy Spraggett from England. Miss Pamela Brady, another nurse from England, had just been appointed to our field; also Dorothy Moos from America.

A fine Christian doctor, Dr. Stuart Harverson, missionary from Hong Kong, felt a great burden to leave his own flourishing Tuberculosis Sanitarium and Clinic and was coming to join us in Viet Nam. His wife would soon follow him here, and the services of this experienced, devoted, spiritual physician and his wife were to mean much to the work of God here in Viet Nam.

Others were looking this way and we were filled with joy at their response and for answered prayer. These missionaries would man some of the jungle beach-heads, but there were many more of the strategic positions still waiting for dozens of more Crusaders.

► 18 ◄

Establishing Work in Kontum Province

THE NEW YEAR OF 1960 brought great happiness to us. We went down to Saigon to meet some of the new missionaries arriving. Dr. Harverson came from Hong Kong bringing his Volkswagon and he purchased a second-hand Land Rover in Saigon. At about the same time, Roy Spraggett came by air from England.

Then our own son and daughter-in-law, Stanley and Ginny, came sailing up the Saigon River, in a sky blue Maersk Boat from Los Angeles. Leslie stood with Gordon and me in the shade of a go-down as we watched the cream-colored super-structure of the bright blue ship appear in the twisting Saigon River. As it drew near us, we could see Stanley up on the bridge, seeing everything with his binoculars but us! It was too blisteringly hot for us to stand out on the dock in the noonday sun.

Finally the pretty blue boat turned slowly and docked, with Stan and Ginny sighting us now and we soon clambered up the gang-plank and were in the arms of our beloved children. What a thrill to welcome them to Viet Nam as missionaries!

We all drove joyfully home the 600 miles from Saigon to Da Nang in Dr. Harverson's two cars.

These new missionaries were soon all digging in with the others, studying the difficult Vietnamese language with teachers.

In February, Dorothy Moos came from Spokane, Washington, and a little later, Pamela Brady, a nurse, came from England. Miss Beryl Smith soon arrived from Australia and Mr. Ulrich Welder came from Germany.

Our staff now numbered 14 foreign missionaries. We met every morning, but Sunday, at our home for an hour of hymns, Bible reading and prayer at 7:30 A.M. On week-ends most of us were out in two or three carloads visiting the stations.

For over twenty years we had prayed and believed that God would give us the privilege of reaching the great mountain tribe, the Jeh. This responsibility had often weighed upon us.

When Gordon was able to open Dak Sut among the Sedang, Halang and Jeh tribes, putting Mr. Tuu and his family there to preach, he saw American bulldozers and scrapers crawling slowly northward from Dak Sut to reopen the old French road to Dak Gle, a Jeh center that he had visited over twenty years previously. The Government Public-Works men would be making a new road straight north that would join up with Phuoc Son (by a side road) and Thanh My and Da Nang.

Some months later, when Gordon, with Dr. Harverson and Roy Spraggett next visited the Tuu family at Dak Sut, they were glad to hear that the road was now open to Dak Gle. So they sped on with happy hearts and praises to God. They thanked Him for the American Aid which is making possible, by bulldozers, machinery and American advisors, the entering of this vast hinterland. How happy we were to follow right behind the big bulldozers and scrapers as they opened the way! As the men traveled north they were amazed to see the splendid new road carved out of the hillsides, up the valleys, and climbing to 3,550 feet at Dak Gle.

Many times as Gordon flew the air-route from Saigon to Da Nang which passes over this hinterland of unreached tribes, he had prayed and wept and sought some way of evangelizing these areas. Now, within the space of a few months, the Americans have helped the Vietnamese to build a highway reaching straight through the heart of this wilderness of mountains and valleys.

They reached Dak Gle and found the new main road was cutting off eight miles below this post to follow an easier valley route.

At Dak Gle the men couldn't see a trace of the early French fort that Gordon had visited here, years before. All had been destroyed in the Viet Minh war. A small detachment of Vietnamese soldiers was camped in a house overlooking the great valley. Half-a-dozen Jeh longhouses clung to the steep hillside nearby. More dotted the valley floor below.

A friendly Jeh who spoke a few words of French, having been in the army in past days, took the men to visit some long-houses. Worse than pigsties, these could hardly be called human habitations. The people were filthy, clad in a few dirty rags in the cold mountain air.

The men stood on a cleared-off shelf of land overlooking the great mountain ranges of Jeh-land — expansive masses of mighty mountains, towering up to pierce the blue sky, with the sunlight and shadows playing over the great green, blue and purple heights and valleys. Here in these silent, mighty, ancient ranges live the poor Jeh people, in their huddling bunches of dejected, ugly, low bamboo and thatched shacks, in misery and neglect all through the centuries.

The men back-tracked from Dak Gle to where the new road was being made. Across a valley they saw the road-builders' temporary camp on a flattened ridge. They waited for the bulldozer to carve out a hillside to smooth a way for the Land Rover to reach the camp. A hundred yards across the ravine, the Jeh village of Dak Rotah nestled on a similar ledge. With tear-filled, shining eyes, Dr. Harverson quietly said, "These are the places God has been calling me to." For 25 years, first as a missionary doctor in Lisu-land, China; then the war years in Africa with the British Army; then nine years in his own flourishing clinic and 70-bed tuberculosis Sanitarium in Hong Kong; God had been preparing him, he felt, for just such a task as this. The call to these poor, unreached tribes had been so great that he had turned over his Hong Kong medical work to others and came to help those who had never heard of Christ, and who had never seen a doctor. He was 52 years old. Mrs. Harverson was finishing the work of getting the Hong Kong hospital settled into the hands of another good group, and she would soon be here to join her husband.

The men began to make plans for Dr. Harverson and Oliver Trebilco, from Australia, and a Vietnamese evangelist, to all start working now at Dak Rotah. They talked with the Vietnamese

District Director of Public Works in his jeep. He asked, "You would like to have a bamboo house here? Of course — my bull-dozer will make a road to it and level the ground."

So the location was decided and orders for the simple house given immediately. The hut on the cleared-off promontory of land would be ready for Dr. Harverson and Oliver in two weeks' time.

On this trip, the doctor began right away to help the people. One young Jeh man by the roadside beckoned to the men in the car for help. Blood was pouring from a deep cut made by a sharp bamboo in his knee. The doctor sutured him by the way-side, with a dozen of the young man's Jeh companions watching. He also treated a man with a septic big toe, and gave him an injection of penicillin.

A Vietnamese student-preacher, Mr. Hanh and his wife, volunteered to be the first missionaries to enter Dak Rotah.

It is hard for these Vietnamese workers to live in a high altitude like this of 3,500 feet. The winds and rain sweep through the woven bamboo walls of the houses, and they shiver in the damp and cold. They leave behind their own yellow-skinned people on the coastal plains to live among the brown-skinned tribespeople up in these mountains and they must learn to speak the tribal language.

But the Jeh men and women, boys and girls of Dak Rotah were friendly and came running down the steep bank to the road and helped carry the belongings of the Vietnamese preacher up to the new station, only a few feet away from their own long-houses.

We have found that these poor Jeh are perhaps the most filthy, degraded and neglected of all the different tribespeople. They seldom wash for fear of offending the spirits and getting sick, so everyone is covered with soot and grime and their few clothes are dirty rags. The babies play in the mud like little pigs in their sties, naked and wild-looking with matted hair.

In two weeks' time, Dr. Harverson and Oliver Trebilco moved into the bamboo thatched shack with a mud floor, made for them at Dak Rotah. This Jeh village in the mountains is in sight of the high Laos Border Range and is 400 miles away from Da Nang.

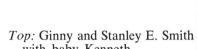

Top: Ginny and Stanley E. Smith with baby Kenneth.

Left: Four tall, sharpened bamboo fences barricade the Jeh tribal resettlement village near Dak Sut against communist attacks.

Below: The Sedang village of Dak Sut, Stanley Smith's district.

Above: Jeh tribeswomen and children at Cak Pek. The Jeh are a primitive, dirty people.
Below: Jeh tribesmen huddle in their blankets in the cold, mountain air.

Top: Dak Rotah station is situated on this shelf above the valleys. This station was later burned by the communists.

Left: Land Rover follows right behind bulldozers opening way into primitive tribal areas.

Below: Bulldozer carves road out of mountainside near Dak Rotah.

Top: Dr. Harverson helps Jeh boy with badly cut knee.

Right: Mr. Tuu, fine Vietnamese preacher, at right, and Jeh Christian worker at Dak Sut.

Below: Roy Spraggett (seated in foreground) and Dr. Harverson with Jeh tribespeople at Dak Rotah.

The nearest market place and post office is Kontum, 100 miles from Dak Rotah. The men would have to live on rice, scrawny chicken and eggs that they could buy from the Jeh. They took up some canned goods to help out. But when this new interior road will be finished it will link up Dak Rotah with Da Nang, a distance of only 125 miles.

It was distressing that the Communists were infiltrating badly into these mountains now from the Laos border only 15 miles away.

Dr. Harverson and Oliver were able to stay at Dak Rotah for only three weeks. One night their little bamboo hut was almost burned down by someone setting fire to bundles of thatch-grass right near the wall where Oliver was sleeping. They put out the fire in time and saw that the thatch-grass had been soaked in kerosene before-hand. Was it the Communists who had set the fire? The government authorities in Kontum became anxious and requested that Dr. Harverson and Oliver leave Dak Rotah as they couldn't guarantee their safety. The Vietnamese missionaries could stay on.

This was disappointing to Dr. Harverson and Oliver, but Gordon immediately got them permission from the government to let them move into Bato, the important station among the great Hrey tribe. They would go there to live as soon as they got a house built, and would start putting this Hrey language into writing; minister to the sick and help the Vietnamese and Hrey workers to evangelize.

Dr. Harverson's and Oliver's influence on the Jeh people, during their three weeks among them, was good and these missionaries will never be forgotten by those tribespeople.

Several months later, Gordon and Stanley took another trip up to this Kontum area. They drove two cars — Stanley driving our old Land Rover and Gordon driving our new diesel-engined Land Rover pick-up, with a small box-trailer behind. They were loaded down, for they were taking more Vietnamese evangelists with their wives, babies and belongings up to occupy stations in this District.

One couple, Mr. and Mrs. Ky, would open up the new station at Plateau G.I., among the 4000 Mnom tribespeople. Mr. Thuong would go to live with the Tuu family at Dak Sut; Mr. Tri would join the Hanh family at Dak Rotah and Mr. and Mrs. An would open up Dak Gle. Mr. Nhut, our Vietnamese Superintendent, was also along on the trip. He and Gordon had decided to put these Vietnamese workers out two by two in these outposts, for it is difficult for them to go on trips out into the dangerous mountains by themselves and to leave their wives and children all alone in these wild places.

They drove up the new military road again from the Bato, Gia Vuc valley, climbing the steep grades and following the narrow ledges blasted out of the rocky faces of the mountains. Even in the eighth lowest gear in four-wheel drive, it was all they could do to get the heavily loaded cars and trailer up the steep hair-pin turns, with the crumbling shoulders and dizzy drops far below them. It would take only a slight skid to send the car over the edge.

But how wonderful it was that the new road has opened up this new tribe's country to the Gospel. Not one of the tribes in this area had heard of Christ until our workers got there.

Gordon, Stanley and Mr. Nhut visited the District Administrator at Plateau G.I., a Jarai tribesman, and decided on buying a little house for the Ky family. They left these young Vietnamese missionaries there, willing to sacrifice and settle down to preach among the Mnom in this wild, new post.

The men continued on to Kontum, where they visited with Mr. and Mrs. Kinh and got authorization to place the three other preachers.

Next day they drove to Dak Sut and left Thuong with Mr. and Mrs. Tuu. These were all valuable workers who would do a good job in this area.

Then they went on to Dak Rotah and placed Tri with the Hanhs. Mr. An and his family would also stay on in Dak Rotah until he could get a house built at Dak Gle, eight miles away over the mountains.

That evening in Dak Rotah the men entered the communal room in the middle of a Jeh longhouse to talk to the crowd of men squatting around the log-fire. The roof was lacquered a shiny black from the smoke-fires and was full of cob-webs and filth. Drums, tobacco leaves and corn cobs were hanging from the rafters. Around the walls there were sixty skulls of water-buffaloes sacrificed during the preceding months for the people's health. All was dim and the smoke smarted the eyes. Gordon held a flashlight on a picture-roll while Mr. Nhut preached through a Jeh interpreter who knew some Vietnamese.

The tribespeople all wanted to believe on Jesus, they said, but they could never give up their sacrifices. "We would get sick and die, if we did," they shouted.

Gordon replied, "You have recently sacrificed sixty water buffaloes and yet people have died during the past few days and another is about to die in that next room. The offerings of the animals and their blood to the spirits are of no avail."

It will take a lot of patient teaching and much prayer and tears to win these wild Jeh people. But the men were happy that they were not hostile to them or to the great Message. Our workers would have good malaria pills to heal their terrible fevers, and sulpha drugs for their dysentery and pneumonia.

As Stanley was on this trip he said he felt that God was calling him and Ginny to settle in this vast Kontum area. Later they would move up to Kontum to help oversee all of this great work.

The new missionaries enjoyed going out with us and the Vietnamese students on week-ends to visit our centers. We went to Phuoc Son, Son Ha, Gi Liang and Dong Ke and held meetings in all of these places. Near Dong Ke, a group of new Christians had started up, about thirty miles away, in a settlement far back in the rice fields, called Son Nam. Over 60 Vietnamese back-settlers there had been won to God through our native evangelists, Mr. Thanh and Mr. Khiem, and especially by one of their new converts, Mr. Soc, who was now in his first year of Bible School. We were greatly encouraged as we visited this fine group of new Christians. Soon the witness spread to another village called Tu My, near there, and around sixty more believed in this place. Today we have Vietnamese evangelists stationed in these two villages, with churches built and the Christians going on with God.

We visited Bong Mieu where Mr. and Mrs. Cang were winning Vietnamese and Cua tribespeople to the Lord. We were there when their fine new bamboo and wooden church was dedicated to God. It was built mostly by the Christians themselves along with a gift from a friend in America.

Now the Gospel had spread from Bong Mieu to the center of An Trung, five miles away. We drove as far as we could and then walked in over the rice-field dikes and up hills for three miles to visit this group. We found around fifty or more bright believers there. One of these had come in some months previously to Da Nang to have his eyes operated on for cataracts by Dr. Strausse, a prominent eye-specialist, from Reading, Pennsylvania. Dr. Strausse and his wife had come out to Da Nang to visit Dr. and Mrs. Billman, and while they were here for three weeks, Dr. Strausse did two hundred free eye operations in Da Nang and Hue! The operation on the Christian man from An Trung was a great success and he returned to his village rejoicing in the healing of his eyes and witnessing for God. As a result of his testimony and the preaching of Cang, this group of people had accepted Christ and were ready to build a chapel in their village.

▶ 19 ◀

Preacher Buried Alive

FOR TWO YEARS, OUR Vietnamese evangelists, Mr. and Mrs. Hiep
and their five children, had ministered in the market town of
Bang Lang, six miles out of Hue. Here the Pakoh tribespeople
came to trade. Mr. Hiep had had one year in our Bible School
and he and his wife were spiritual and both were always giving
an earnest, enthusiastic witness for Christ. They each had taken
the Correspondence Bible Course put out by The Navigators in
Saigon and had obtained their certificates.

One week-end, Gordon and I were out camping with them in
their little bamboo chapel at Bang Lang, and at the night meeting
a dozen or so Pakoh tribespeople came in and sat down on the
benches. They were led by their old chieftain and were from a
village called Khe Tranh, eleven miles out in the jungle from
Bang Lang. This chief had acted, until recently, as representative
to the government for the Pakoh tribes. Hiep had been witnessing to them at the market place and had visited in their village.
This night as we showed several fine new picture rolls on the
Life, Death and Resurrection of Christ, they were all deeply
touched and led by the old chief, they all prayed – the first Pakoh
tribespeople to accept Jesus as their Saviour.

After that, Hiep and his wife often visited their village and
Gordon, also, made some trips out there. They would go up the
river from Bang Lang by sampan for five miles, or so, and then
would walk six miles through the jungle to this village of Khe
Tranh. The whole village of around twenty adults and a number
of children accepted Christ and gave up their animal sacrifices and
old heathen ways. They were anxious to have their own chapel

162

and wanted Mr. Hiep to come and live with them as their own pastor.

Dr. and Mrs. Billman took some money that had been given to them toward buying a car and gave it to Mr. Hiep for the building of the bamboo and thatch chapel at Khe Tranh. The Hieps, with their oldest daughter and their baby, then lived there in rooms at the back of the chapel most of the time, just going in now and then to Bang Lang to minister in the chapel-house there. The other three children stayed in Bang Lang, all by themselves, to go to school there and care for the house. They were two little girls, just ten and seven years old and their five-year-old brother.

The little girls bought their own food at the market, cooked it, cared for their little brother and the house. The neighbors were kind to them. Now and then the three little tots walked the eleven miles, all alone, over the tiger, leopard and wild-elephant infested jungle-road to visit their family and carry out some food supplies to them. What heroic children they were! We asked these tiny ones if they were ever afraid, and they answered simply, "Why should we be afraid? Jesus is with us!"

One week-end, Joan Burridge, Beryl Smith, Mr. Nhut, Gordon and I visited the Hieps out at the Khe Tranh village. A road, passable for cars, had been built out there now from Bang Lang, especially for woodcutters. This road would eventually reach to the Laotian border at A Luoi, fifty miles away. We missionaries were able to drive out on this trail.

We had an enjoyable time visiting with the Pakoh Christians in their little village, preaching to them. Joan, the nurse, ministered to their physical needs. The good old chief always did the translating for us from the Vietnamese language into Pakoh. We visited in each of their homes and planned to have the chief's granddaughter, Mua, an especially bright, attractive girl, who spoke and wrote Vietnamese well, to go in to the Hue Hospital to study nursing.

The new chapel was up on a hill overlooking the village some 200 yards away. There was a river with a lovely deep swimming-hole in it and we had fun bathing there with the children. Mrs. Hiep had planted a nice garden around the chapel and she gave us corn, fresh from her little field and sweet potatoes and onions.

WAGGONER CHRISTIAN CHURCH

Right: Preacher Hiep and family.
Left: Pakoh tribal chief and Hiep — both martyrs for Christ, murdered by the communists.
Below: Mua's home in Khe Tranh village.

Top: Pakoh chapel later burned by communists.
Right: Mua, the lovely Pakoh girl, who was buried alive by the communists.

Below: Land Rover and wood-cutter's truck meet on the jungle trail to Khe Tranh.

Each night we had a good meeting in the chapel. Hiep had built a bamboo "guest house" by the side of the road as a stop-over place for visiting tribespeople on their long journeys to and from the interior, some eight days' walk away. There were more than twenty in the guest-house at this time, on their way from villages back as far as A Luoi. They came to our meetings and were wild-looking tribespeople — naked except for loin-cloths — with long, tangled hair.

They listened well to the Gospel and one night six of them came forward and prayed to God.

We returned home rejoicing in the way God was working in this Khe Tranh center.

Then three weeks later tragedy struck! At 10:20 p.m. on September 6, 1960, a band of twelve armed Communist guerillas came to the little undefended jungle outpost. Mr. and Mrs. Hiep and baby were asleep in their little room at the back of the chapel. Four of the Communists pounded on the chapel door crying, "We want Hiep! We want Hiep!" Mr. Hiep got up and opened the door.

The Communists threw a rope around Hiep's neck and told him he must go with them. One slashed the tires on Hiep's mission bicycle so it could not be used to call for help. They didn't take Mrs. Hiep or her baby — perhaps because Mrs. Hiep is so tiny and frail-looking. Fortunately the oldest daughter, fourteen years old, had gone in with the three other children to Bang Lang market for supplies.

The Communists led Hiep away with the rope around his neck. They let him take his raincoat, but nothing else, not even his Bible.

Four more guerillas entered the guest house and caught a Vietnamese woodcutter, but after telling him not to work any more for the Catholic priests who were supposedly exploiting the timber for their own personal benefit, they let him go.

At the same time four other Communists entered the little Christian village of Khe Tranh. They told the Christian chief to follow them, but he refused. So they tried to shoot him, but their pistol would not go off. Then they grabbed him, strangled him and threw him down on the ground dead.

They then captured the chief's beautiful granddaughter, Mua, and put a rope around her neck. They marched her and Mr. Hiep off into the night.

Word reached the Vietnamese Administrator at Bang Lang next day and he had the soldiers of the fort take out a truck and bring Mrs. Hiep and the baby and some of their belongings back to our little chapelhouse in Bang Lang.

We, at Da Nang, didn't hear of the attack until three days later. Immediately, Gordon and Dr. Harverson drove the seventy miles up to Bang Lang, arriving at 8 P.M. They found a crowd of sympathetic Vietnamese around Mrs. Hiep's house. They tried to comfort Mrs. Hiep and the children who were overcome with grief. Her first thought was, *How soon could we send another preacher to replace her husband?* "I'll walk back there to Khe Tranh the eleven miles with him each week-end to help look after the work," she said. For her, the work came first and we knew that Hiep, too, as much as possible, would be bearing witness to his Saviour.

The neighbors were kind in bringing her and her family some food and help.

The next morning, Gordon saw the Administrator and he told Gordon that he was going to try to find Mr. Hiep, but having such an immense territory of jungle and mountain, he feared it would be almost impossible.

Gordon and Dr. Harverson drove in to Khe Tranh and the Administrator insisted that they take four armed soldiers in the Land Rover with them.

As they walked into the little village, the poor tribal Christians were sitting on the bamboo floors, holding their children, peering mutely out of the windows. "We can't eat or sleep," they numbly said, with tears pouring over their faces.

Gordon and Dr. Harverson gathered them together for consolation and prayer and they all prayed in their Pakoh language — women, children and men — each one fervently calling on God for help. They are just young Christians and this was a frightful test for their faith. We all upheld them in prayer.

With the soldiers guarding them, Gordon and Dr. Harverson had lunch under a tree, gathered up a few more of the poor belongings of the Hieps, and the Christians said they would take care of the Chapel until Mr. Hiep would come back.

As the men drove away, they looked up at the bravely worded sign in Vietnamese and English, "THE WORLDWIDE EVANGELIZATION CRUSADE." How desolate the station was now, made so by the atheistic, anti-God, anti-Christ Communists.

A few weeks later we heard that the authorities had caught some of the assassins. We hurried up to Bang Lang to hear the story.

The Administrator told us that some of the Communist tribespeople who had helped capture Hiep had been caught. The military beat them until they talked and told the whole story. They said Hiep and the girl, Mua, had been made to walk five days back into the mountains to A-Luoi near the Laos border. Then they buried them alive in separate graves! Two government soldiers, who had tried to defend them, were also buried alive together in another grave — all four were buried at the same time. The reason given for this atrocity was that these people were "American Imperialist Agents" working for the Americans. A week or so before her capture, Mua had helped a Wycliffe translator, who had now come to Hue to work on putting this Pakoh tribal language into writing. He had visited this Christian village and as Mua knew Vietnamese quite well, she had helped him for two hours to write down some of her Pakoh language.

She was a very pretty girl of nineteen years, the very light and life of Khe Tranh. She could have been a help to the Wycliffe workers, and she would have been an intelligent nurse and worker for the Lord. Her teeth had never been hacked out like the other girls of her tribe, and they were pearly and even.

Her parents, among the leading Christians of her village, were stricken with grief.

The Vietnamese Administration had the whole Pakoh village of Khe Tranh moved in near Bang Lang for protection, and later the Communists completely destroyed our little chapel on the hill.

Mrs. Hiep and her children have remained on in Bang Lang to this day, where they are giving a fine witness for the Lord and where she can help the Pakoh Christians who have come in from the jungles. The Christian Children's Fund from America very kindly took this widow and her family of five under their care —

building her a nice little brick house in Bang Lang, with a garden, and sending her support each month. The children are all in school.

Our Bible students took this all very soberly, realizing what might be in store for them, also, in days to come. As we showed them dear Mr. Hiep's photo, one young man, called Minh, jumped to his feet and said, "I'll go and take his place. I'm not afraid to die!"

Today, Minh and his bright young wife and two little girls are doing a fine piece of work for God at the Bang Lang Chapel.

> When we shall stand within the court of heaven,
> Where white-robed pilgrims pass before our sight;
> Earth's martyred saints and blood-washed overcomers —
> These then are they who walk with Him in white.
> O to be worthy then to stand beside them,
> And in that morn to walk with Him in white.

▶ 20 ◀

Tragedy at Dak Rotah

DAK ROTAH! — A NAME THAT meant much to us early in the year
of 1960. It meant the splendid new highway being cut through
the heart of Viet Nam, bringing this Jeh village and the Jeh tribe
within reach of the missionary. It meant the outpost "the farthest
into the night." It meant the most degraded of all our mountain
people. It meant the first W.E.C. out-station to be named by
foreign missionaries.

After Dr. Harverson and Oliver Trebilco had to leave this dangerous post in May, Mr. Hanh and his family, and Mr. Tri, carried on, living in a bamboo house and using the missionaries' hut
for a chapel. The An family was also living there until they could
get settled in Dak Gle. Four of the Jeh tribespeople had prayed
to God and the Vietnamese workers were teaching thirty of the
Jeh young people and children to sing "Jesus Loves Me" and other
hymns.

It was now the month of October and they were beginning to
practice some of the Christmas hymns — "Away in a Manger,"
and "Silent Night" — and were planning for the first Christmas
program for the Jeh.

Sickness attacked our workers there. Mrs. An came down with
typhoid fever and had to be taken in to the Kontum hospital. Tri
got malaria badly and ulcers of the mouth.

A dysentery epidemic broke out among the Jeh and the people
were dying all around with the disease. Ten died within a short
time. Because of their superstitions, they did not bury their dead,
but placed them down the hill below our preachers' hut, where
the stench became unbearable.

The Vietnamese workers could hardly sleep at night for the continual beating of gongs and booming of drums, as the Jeh offered their sacrifices to the evil spirits for the healing of their sick.

Then one day, we received a telegram from Kontum saying that Hoa (meaning "Flower") had passed away. She was the little daughter of Mr. and Mrs. Hanh. She had had dysentery badly. The road now was so terrible with rains and floods that the Public Works trucks had not been able to get through to Kontum, one hundred miles away. After a week, they finally were able to take the child out by truck but she died on the road. The torrential rains, deep mud, the terrible jolting of the truck through ruts and holes, no doubt contributed to hastening the end of this dear little girl.

The three preachers came back to Da Nang for a few days to tell us of all their sorrows and then, strengthened, they returned to Dak Rotah and the work again. At this time they left their wives and children in Kontum with Mr. and Mrs. Kinh and the wives attended the Government Hospital each day to learn something about the simple treatment of diseases. They would remain in Kontum until the heavy rains and the epidemic of sickness and death in Dak Rotah should cease.

The clouds billowed up the mountain passes bringing bone-chilling dampness. With the cold winds swirling around their bamboo hut, our Vietnamese preachers bundled up and huddled close around their open wood fire. The rains slashed through the woven bamboo walls and the mud floor was slippery and never dry.

During the night of October 19, someone tried to get into the Hanh's thatched house, but whoever it was, ran away when soldiers in the nearby fort opened fire. Two hundred government troops were now guarding Dak Rotah and our workers had felt safe there.

However, the next morning, after the night of the attempted entrance to the hut, feeling that danger was near, Mr. Hanh got on his bicycle and rode the one hundred miles into Kontum.

In the early morning of October 21, at 4 A.M., the Communists, made up of Vietnamese, Laotians, and tribesmen, swept out of the jungle and attacked Dak Rotah! They began to burn all

Top: Public works road-building equipment and camp at Dak Rotah.
Below: Jeh children learning to sing "Jesus Loves Me" before communists destroyed Dak Rotah and all had to flee.

the buildings. Our bamboo house and chapel soon went up in smoke! They burned the new bamboo government schoolhouse and they over-ran the two forts. The two hundred Vietnamese soldiers fled into the woods, many being taken prisoner.

The Communists caught Mr. Tri and tied his hands behind his back and kept a guard over him in one of the forts with nine Vietnamese soldiers also taken prisoners.

They chased the tribespeople out of their houses and told them to run into the mountains. Then they burned up the entire Jeh village. Bamboo and thatch-grass burn very quickly. They made Tri and the other prisoners they had caught go ahead on a jungle path while they held guns to their backs.

They had also captured our evangelist, Mr. An, and they marched him off, with more soldier prisoners, in another direction. They had no rope to tie An's hands and before they had time to get thongs for him, some of the Vietnamese national soldiers rallied and began firing at the Communists. During all the activity and excitement, An escaped into the jungle. Nearby was a roaring waterfall and he knew of a place where he could hide behind it. He stayed there until, in the midst of all the shooting, he was able to creep away unnoticed. Then he kept on running, hiding in crevices, rocks, valleys, and they didn't catch him.

The battle at Dak Rotah lasted for eight hours, from 4 A.M. to noon. There was a dreadful slaughter of the Vietnamese troops. The Public Works camp, and both the forts, and all of Dak Rotah were completely destroyed.

Mr. An climbed a tree to try to get his bearings in the mountain wilderness. God helped him to see a lone Vietnamese Public Works man running through the jungle, coming his way. He, too, was escaping from the Communists. An joined up with him and this helped save An's life for the road-builder knew something of the way out of the wild country. Without him, An could have been lost. They worked their way for two days and a night through the valleys and over the mountains, always afraid of meeting Communist guerillas. They just had leaves to eat and once they found a green pumpkin in a tribal field. They did not dare to go near any tribal village for fear that the Communists might be hiding there. They slept out at night in great danger of tigers and wild beasts. By a long, round-about way they finally came out at the Public Works' Station at Dak Pek, another Jeh center, fifteen miles south on the road leading to Dak Sut and Kontum. They were able to get on a Public Works truck there and ride in to Kontum in safety.

Mr. and Mrs. Kinh and An's wife and children joyously received him and cared for him. Then he got on a native bus and rode the two days' trip to Da Nang bringing us the news!

When he reached us he was still all scratched up from the forest brambles and was very tired. Every now and then he'd stop telling his story to praise the Lord and say, "I'm alive today only by the grace of God!"

We were greatly shaken up over it all! — and Tri was still missing! Our minds turned immediately to the news we had just received the week before of Hiep's and Mua's cruel deaths and we wondered if Tri would be next!

How glad we were that the women and children and Mr. Hanh from Dak Rotah were all safe in Kontum.

Our minds flew to our missionaries, some of whom were now out on stations. Dr. and Mrs. Harverson and Oliver Trebilco were already living in their new little brick cottage at Bato learning the Hrey language. It was not so dangerous there but still they were in need of much prayer as the Communists were closing in.

Dr. Harverson said, "We will stay on here in the midst of this great Hrey tribe at Bato, even if the Communists come and kill us."

Two hundred Communists were swarming in the vicinity. Nearly every night they would even come in the dark to a hilltop near the doctor's little house and would call out their propaganda, telling the people to leave the government and join them and giving many warnings. The doctor said, "They are like Goliath challenging the Israelites. But if they come in and have a battle, I'll be here to care for the wounded."

He and his wife were willing to live dangerously for God. They were getting on in their fifties but they are young and brave in spirit before this thrilling work they are doing.

Joan Burridge, the nurse, and Daphne Lydamore had gone out to our station at Thanh My and were living in the little chapel there and, along with the native evangelist, were ministering to the Vietnamese and Katu tribespeople. They were the only white people in that lonely center, sixty miles from Da Nang.

Dr. and Mrs. Billman and children had been living at Bana for several months now. The leprosy patients and Mr. Yen, the Vietnamese Director, had cleared off a plot of ground and we put up some long brick buildings, and had water running in pipes from a spring.

Mrs. Billman had had a recurrence of tuberculosis, which she had had in Africa, and was forced to have complete rest and quiet. So they had moved out to the lovely Bana property in the jungle-clad hills where Mrs. Billman soon grew better.

But the Communists were coming now to the Katu villages up in the foothills of Bana mountain tempting the tribespeople to follow them. Would the Billmans be safe there much longer?

The little group of Jeh tribespeople at Dak Rotah, who had prayed to Christ, and the young people and little children who had been learning Christmas hymns and Bible verses for the Christmas program, were all scattered. Dak Rotah was a smouldering ruin. Even the several other Jeh villages near Dak Rotah had all been burned. Hundreds of the poor Jeh people were now left homeless — out in the wildest jungles, in this, the coldest, rainiest time of the year, and many of them were still suffering with the dysentery epidemic. Saddest of all, they were still out in the darkness, without the Gospel. Only a few had let a little of the light shine through to them.

The Communist guerillas were now all through the mountain areas of Viet Nam. They were assassinating many government officials and were enticing thousands of tribespeople from each of the different tribes, to leave their villages and follow them into the hills. They promised the tribespeople nice clothing, wristwatches, fountain pens — great treasures to the poor people — but they would be in for big disillusionments.

We were not hindered from traveling on most of the roads to visit our twenty-eight stations, but it was now unsafe for the missionaries to go back any distance into the jungles, owing to the presence of the guerillas.

But the doors were certainly *not* closing to missionary work! This was no time for a defeatist attitude.

For twenty years, missionaries out here in Viet Nam had been going through dangerous times — ever since the Japanese invasion of Viet Nam in 1941, and then through the terrible years of the French-Viet Minh Communist war from 1946 to 1954. Most of the missionaries had been in potential danger throughout these years.

Despite all this, since 1956, God had enabled us to advance under the W.E.C. into these new areas, until by now, we had occupied nearly every strategic tribal center in Central Viet Nam.

But we could not now call any of our stations safe from attack and so we leaned heavily upon the precious prayers and faith of our friends in the homelands.

After several days of anxiety and much prayer for Tri, a telegram came from Kontum! Good news! God had miraculously delivered Tri, as He had An. Tri, now, was safe in Kontum!

A volume of rejoicing went up to the Lord, who had brought Tri back to us!

A few days later, he and Mr. Thuong from Dak Sut arrived by native bus in Da Nang. As we met with Tri, we had the same feeling that I am sure the Christians of old must have experienced when Peter was delivered from prison and appeared to them. What a thrill it was to hear of God's deliverance!

Tri told us of how he had been in the hands of the Communists for two days and two nights. They had kept him in the fort for one hour at Dak Rotah, all tied up, along with nine captured Vietnamese soldiers, while they continued shooting at the escaped soldiers. They asked Tri about his religion. What were his ideals and purposes and his field of work as a pastor? They said he had to go with them because he was working for the Americans. They would teach him the Communist doctrines.

They made Tri and the other prisoners go ahead of them with guns pointing at their backs. Tri said he was afraid at first, but he kept crying to God and after a few hours, the fear left him. As they had him a prisoner for these days and nights, the Communists asked him, "Why aren't you worried?"

Tri answered, "I have Jesus Christ. I do not worry. I am praying to God all the time. He will set me free."

Tri told us, "I was not sad. I smiled as I ate the rice and salt they gave me. I smiled as I spoke to the Communists. I could even sleep well. The other prisoners were afraid and cried, 'The Communists will kill us!' But I told them that I was not afraid. If they wanted to kill me that was all right. I was not afraid to die, for I have Jesus, my Saviour, and He would take me to heaven. If God willed me to die, I'll die. If God willed me to live, He would save me. I was not afraid."

He preached to the prisoners about Christ. The captive who slept beside him on the mountain-side said, "I'd like to believe on Jesus too."

Then on October 24, after three days' marching as prisoners, they heard the planes and rumbling trucks and armored cars coming from Kontum. Five hundred soldiers were brought to Dak Rotah. The Communists had put thousands of poisoned lances all along the path behind them to keep the soldiers from following them. But they realized that these well-equipped soldiers from Kontum could clear the spikes away with big special shovels they had for this. So they began to fear and they finally said to Tri and the other nine soldiers, "We will let you all go now."

They unleashed their hands, and the Vietnamese soldiers could lead Tri back over the mountains to Dak Rotah without following the path full of poisoned lances. They climbed and descended the many miles back and finally reached the ruined fort. Tri was sad to see that all the buildings were burned and he and the other preachers had lost their Bibles, hymn-books, picture rolls and all their clothing. Their precious tribe Christians and the children were gone!

Thuong, from Dak Sut, gave us the report of his and Mr. Tuu's station. Some of the tribespeople there had now prayed. Thuong had gone preaching right up to the border of Laos. One day as he was witnessing in a bamboo longhouse, built low down on the ground, a tiger came dashing right through one of the low doors chasing a dog! Thuong and the others, exceedingly frightened, made a great noise and the tiger ran out again!

Thuong told us that Communist guerillas up in this section

have their teeth sawed off to the gums, and put plugs in their ear-
lobes to disguise themselves as tribespeople. They were inter-
marrying with the tribal girls.

The Communists attacked Plateau G.I. and killed the Administrator, who was a Jarai tribesman and who had been friendly and
helpful to us in establishing the work there. The place was partly
destroyed and the Ky family just got out with their lives. The
military convoy taking them back to Kontum was attacked in a
mountain pass and six people were killed.

The house of the American road builders at Plateau G.I., which
we had visited several times, was destroyed but fortunately the
Americans were in Kontum at the time.

Since then, Plateau G.I. has become a big Vietnamese Army
Camp and several villages of the Mnom tribespeople have been resettled nearby. Road travel there, as yet, is too dangerous, so the
only way to visit Plateau G.I. today is by helicopter. Stanley was
recently flown in by American military friends. We hope to be
able to put a preacher there soon and rebuild this station.

▶ 21 ◀

First Attack on Tra Bong

AT ABOUT THE SAME TIME that the Communists demolished Dak Rotah, they also attacked Tra Bong. At 3:30 A.M. on October 17, 1960, they came, one hundred strong, roaring into our chapel ground which was right beside the Government Administration offices and the fort. They had ladders to climb over the hedges and high bamboo fences and they quickly hacked their way through, with tremendous blood-curdling yells of "Onward! Go forward!" They wore no shirts — just short trousers and green kerchiefs around their necks. Stars, the Communist sign, made of bamboo, hung down their backs. Some had a camouflage of leaves on their heads.

Our preacher, Cuu, and his wife, two little girls and baby boy, and Quang, our Cua tribes preacher, woke out of their sleep! The Cuu family rushed out of their house attached to the chapel and jumped into a small fox-hole they had dug among their banana trees, a few feet from their house. It was full of mud and water in this rainy season but they crawled back into it and had a hard time to keep the baby from crying out.

Quang had no time to get out of his corner in the chapel house. He just rolled himself up in his dark khaki mosquito net and slid under his bamboo bed in the darkness.

The Communists immediately took over our chapel as a base for attacking the fort. With their ladders they scaled the barbed-wire entanglements and trenches, yelling and shrieking all the time. They began throwing grenades and setting fire to the camp.

The fort was being held by only forty home-guards — just ordinary men of the village who had had a little training. The main

body of soldiers had been divided up into six sections and were
out guarding six different villages, from three to seven miles all
around Tra Bong. They had thought that the Communists would
attack these outlying places. The home-guard had a gun each but
they were only forty men against these one hundred Communists.

The firing, screaming and swirling of the combatants kept up in
the darkness. The Communists set fire to the thatch-roofed buildings in the fort and fought with grenades, bayonets and pistols.

The fire was raging only a few yards from our chapel, but God
miraculously kept it from being destroyed.

The forty home-guards fired back bravely and skillfully from
their trenches. They were killing and wounding some of the Communists. Ten of the home-guard were captured, tied up strongly
and thrown into several pits. The Communists told them that
they would be the ones to hoist the Communist flag over Tra Bong
when the battle would be over.

The soldiers' wives and children were all in the camp too,
crouching down in holes and trenches.

The battle raged for four hours. As dawn began to break, the
attackers were running out of ammunition. One of them now
spied the Cuu family hiding down in their fox-hole. He wanted
to shoot them but he had no cartridges left. He called out to
another Communist to throw a grenade into the hole. But there
were no grenades left. The Communist shouted to still another
to come and shoot into the fox-hole, but he, too, had no more
ammunition. So three times, God delivered the little family! Mrs.
Cuu was terribly frightened and crying, and they had to keep
their hands over the little children's mouths to muffle their cries
from being heard.

The Communists were now fighting with their bayonets, hand
to hand.

Just then twenty more armed home-guards from a post up the
road arrived. They had been guarding that section of the village
but they hadn't been attacked. Now they began to shoot the
Communists and bayonet them. They were full of liquor and
high spirits. They killed sixteen Communists and these were lying
dead all around our chapel. They also wounded many.

The eighty Communists who were left, now had to flee over

the rice fields and up into the mountains. They carried away four of their dead comrades and left the sixteen that were lying in our chapel grounds.

The twenty home-guards who had arrived to deliver the camp now cut the ropes from the ten prisoners.

The brave defenders of the fort had taken seventeen guns from the Communists, one carbine and one Colt pistol.

It was now 7 A.M. and Cuu and his family crawled out of their fox-hole of mud and water. They had been in it since 3:30 A.M. Quang crept out from under his bed and dark mosquito net. He was safe and sound.

The chapel was full of bullet-holes and partly damaged, but they could soon plaster it up again with mud, cement and thatch-grass. Their clothing, cook-pots and wash-basins had been destroyed by the Communists' bullets. But now they all rejoiced in the goodness of God in delivering them and Tra Bong!

At the same time that Tra Bong was attacked, the Communists assaulted five other of the surrounding villages just as the soldiers had predicted. From sixty to seventy Communists attacked each of these places. But the Vietnamese soldiers and home-guards gained the victory in each village — repulsing the Communists and in one place, killing eight of them.

Mr. Cuu was seriously ill for a week after the strain of the battle and exposure in the fox-hole. But he was soon back on the job again at Tra Bong, where he and his dear family and Quang are still carrying on today.

► 22 ◄

We Build a Boat

ONE OF OUR NEW HORIZONS now was to take the Gospel to the islands off the coast of Viet Nam in our section of the country.

One large island, called Ly Son, is one hundred miles from Da Nang and twenty miles out in the sea opposite Quang Ngai. There are seven thousand Vietnamese fishermen on Ly Son Island who have never heard the Gospel and never had medical assistance. Mr. Lich, the first evangelist to visit the island, had gone there by a tiny launch and he said he had such a rough trip that he lay in the bottom of the boat and "died" twice. But he came back with the stirring report of this untouched field. We were greatly burdened to place a Vietnamese worker here soon and to help him get started to evangelize this needy island.

Out in the sea, opposite Da Nang, four hours away by boat, is another island called Cu Lao Cham, where there are three hundred and fifty fishermen who had never heard the Gospel.

So after our arrival back from furlough, Gordon soon signed a contract with some Vietnamese boat-builders who build fishing launches here in Da Nang. Our boat was to be made of heavy hardwood, using great timbers for ribs and keel. It would be fifty feet long, weighing many tons. It would have to be strong and sea-worthy enough to venture out to these off-shore islands. It would have to be weather-proof to protect cargo and people in bad weather and the engine would have to be good and strong for the job.

Soon back in the jungle was heard the sound of axe and saw mingled with cries of "down" and "look out!" as tree after tree was felled and the heavy timbers were sent floating down the river to Da Nang. The Vietnamese workers set up a thatched shed in a meadow, 150 yards from the Da Nang River, opposite the city. The men used the pit method of sawing. The log is leaned against a support and one man stands on top and another underneath, pulling at the long saw together, back and forth. They brought specially shaped logs with natural elbows and bends, that just had to be finished properly to become the ribs and other strong parts of the hull. The planking was 1¾ inches thick, and there was to be a long channel-iron under the 12-inch keel. This keel was a log, 45 feet long, squared off, 8 inches thick and a foot deep.

In Saigon, Gordon purchased a Cummins Diesel Marine engine of 70 h.p. with propeller and shaft, for $2,000.00. The hull, with cabin and pilot house, rudder system, installation of motor and painting, would cost another $2,000. So for about $4,000.00, we were getting a vessel which would cost many times that amount if made in the U.S.A.

On our furlough trip at that time, Gordon had made out a list of items that would be needed for the boat, which he knew would be hard or impossible to obtain in Viet Nam. So as we went along, this is how we secured the parts:

In Toronto, Canada — two boat-hook points.

Kokomo, Indiana — movable searchlight, position lights.

Honolulu — fog-horn, whistle, compass.

Kobe, Japan — brass fittings, cleats, window fasteners, brass runners and wheels for sliding doors and windows, Danforth anchor, wooden steering wheel. (Our cabin on board ship became a bit crowded!)

Hong Kong — brass fittings, hinges.

Since the engine came without instructions or fittings, Gordon had to study where each thing is attached, and had to have made dozens of brass fittings in a little Chinese machine-shop in town. He had to design the cabin, the pilot house, rudder system, fuel and cooling system and many other things about the craft.

It took Gordon and nine workmen four months to make the boat. The workmen were all unskilled, as we know carpenters, using the crudest of tools. Their pay ranged from fifty cents a day, for young apprentices, to eighty cents, and one dollar a day

WAGGONER CHRISTIAN CHURCH

for experienced men. This is why we were able to make it so cheaply. In America, a boat like this would cost nearly $30,000.00.

It meant that Gordon had to be on the job every day to see that work was done according to the plans he had made, for he had designed it to fit our need. In this country, carpenters never use a spirit level, and seldom use a square. They trust to their eye, so that there were always changes to be made and Gordon was continually saying, "You'll have to do this over again — it isn't straight."

When the boat was all painted white, and with a turquoise-blue line around it, we named it, "Hy-Vong" (which means, "Hope") and had the name painted on it.

It was sturdily built to stand rough weather and it floated like a swan. The interior was not fancy but was varnished hardwood. The engine pushes it along at a satisfactory speed of six or seven knots.

We had a fine dedication service for the "Hy-Vong" when it was all finished, and invited various officials, missionaries, workers of the C. and M.A., and other friends. There was quite a crowd and the Mayor of Da Nang was present and made a speech. There was a hymn and a word of explanation from our Vietnamese Chairman, Mr. Nhut, and then a prayer of dedication. We had "dressed the ship" — which means we borrowed a set of signal flags and tied them stem to stern by the top of the mast. The Vietnamese flag flew at the stern pole, and on top of the main flag pole, we flew the Christian flag — red cross on blue, with a white field, which is authorized by the government for our use.

After the ceremony, the Mayor cut the ribbon, and then about forty people clambered aboard for a short sail down the river.

Gordon and some of the Vietnamese workers now made a number of trips to Cu Lao Cham and Ly Son Islands. When the Bible School closed in May, I, too, was able to go.

On my first trip, Gordon, two Vietnamese evangelists, Anh Hai, our Vietnamese pilot, Mr. Nam, and the deckhand, Mr. Tam, were aboard.

Around 9:30 A.M. "Hy-Vong" thrust off from the pier and we began to move smoothly down the Da Nang river. There is much pleasure in the movement of the boat. We have two wicker chairs up in the bow and when it is calm weather this is my favorite place. But when the bow pitches in a fifteen-foot arc, up and down, I soon go to the rear of the boat or lie down in the cabin!

We are down quite close to the water and I love the sound of the ripples lapping against the boat's side with little liquid noises, and the smell of the sea-water.

It was the calm season, from May to the end of September, when the weather is serene and the sea lies dreaming.

We chugged out past the harbor to the great expanse of the ocean. The smooth, sparkling waters were covered with fishing sampans, with their yellow matting sails — sometimes five sails to a boat. There were hundreds of these sailboats within the view far out to sea, for the waters are filled with fish. Sometimes we would pass close to the sampans. The central section of these boats is covered with a semi-circular roof of plaited bamboo, and this is the crew's home. They use the sails cleverly to catch every breath of the gentle breeze. When this fails, they all row, facing forward.

I feasted my eyes upon the marvelous beauty of the sea and boats and great Son Cha mountain on our right. It is a rocky peninsula jutting out for miles into the sea, covered with green jungle growth. On the highest peak, the Americans have now built a big radar station and at the rocky point of the peninsula there is an old French lighthouse.

The cross-currents get a little rough here as we round the cape, and as it was now about noon, we went down below to eat our lunch. Anh Hai gets sea-sick quite easily, and I, too, had to lie down on one of our cozy cabin beds, while Gordon got our lunch together — opening some canned food and pouring coffee from the thermos bottle.

I went back to my chair in the bow when we got past the rough place and enjoyed the smooth trip across to the first Island of Cu Lao Cham.

It is a large mountain, green from base to summit with matted vegetation of forests and festoons of vines, and with many rocks. The beaches are soft golden sand. Surrounding the large island, are six other smaller and rocky ones, adding more beauty to the place.

Missionary boat, *Hy-Vong,* moving down the Da Nang River
toward the open sea.

The *Hy-Vong* floats free after near disaster.

Fishing sampans with
matting sails.

We anchored in deep, clear, blue-green water, a few yards from the beach, in front of the main village which hides under coconut palms. There were a dozen fishing boats, some drawn up on the beaches, others swinging on their anchor ropes. Men were mending nets on the shore. Festoons of these brown and black nets hung drying upon racks erected above the beaches.

We went in to visit the village in our little "life-boat" — a round coracle, like a tub, made of woven bamboo and covered inside and out with pitch. It is unsteady and hard to get in and out of. The Vietnamese use these little tubs a great deal and they can stand heavy seas. Nam or Tam, the boat-men, paddled us in to shore. This takes skill, for the coracle turns round in circles, until one learns how to guide it properly. Gordon soon got on to the way of paddling it. We could look down into the depths of the clear turquoise water and see the craggy coral in places.

The fisher-folk on the island were quite friendly. We went from house to house inviting them to a meeting that evening, and trying to get acquainted with them. The Vietnamese are deeply tanned here as they are out on the sea most of the time. They had seen Gordon when he was here before, but this was the first time they had seen a white woman, so they stared at me with much curiosity. We were the first missionaries ever to come to this island.

After an early supper on the boat, we gathered the villagers together on the sandy beach and showed them many flannelgraphs of the stories of Jesus. They had never heard the Gospel until our evangelists had visited them, so everything was new to them.

Animistic Buddhism had been the religion of this island through the centuries, and the people are full of superstition and their minds are dark and deadened. The moon was out full and with a small kerosene lantern lighting up the pictures, we were able to keep on preaching well into the night. One of the leading Buddhists on the island kept interrupting us as we spoke, but later he admitted that he was only seeking for the truth and was not too sure of his own religion. Others showed quite a lot of interest but felt they didn't understand enough yet to make a decision.

We spent two days and nights here. It was enjoyable living on the "Hy-Vong" with the blue-green water, boats and jungle mountain before our eyes. The warm breeze blew softly through our cabin, scented with blossoms from off-shore and the salt water. The full moon hung overhead flooding the placid nights with silver and the dawns came in a great flush of rose pink. We had some wonderful swimming in warm, crystal water.

These off-shore islands are probably the most peaceful places today in Viet Nam, for there are no Communists here and the people don't have to bother making defenses around their villages, as on the mainland.

In the daytime the people were mostly all away, either fishing out at sea, or tending their meager crops in their little pieces of land at the foot of the mountain, or cutting firewood to sell on the mainland.

We gave out medicines for which the people were very grateful. Many had sore eyes. The second evening we had another good meeting on the beach, sowing more of the precious Gospel Seed.

The following day we made an early start, hoping to make Ly Son Island within eight hours and get there before dark. We followed the shores of the Cu Lao Cham Island and saw a troop of monkeys playing on the sand. We passed another group of Vietnamese houses farther along on a little beach on this same island. On the next trip we would visit this village, too, and preach to those poor people.

The "Hy-Vong" glided through a narrow passage between two steep-sided islands of sheer rock and then we were out in the great circular solitude of the sky and sea again. The coast of Viet Nam was some twenty miles away covered in blue haze.

We had eight wonderful hours gazing out on the quiet blue sea. Gordon and I sat on the chairs up in the front of the boat, wearing our sun-glasses and with umbrellas over our heads. The sun sparkled in a myriad of diamonds and the sea was like liquid blue silk. There was not a trace of foam on the smooth, pure water. The sea was breathing slowly with long, cradling swells.

Now and then flying fish would skim for hundreds of yards with their shiny wings fluttering at a tremendous rate. Some curious two-foot long fish, with narrow silver bodies, would rise up like rockets from the depths and stand almost upright on their tails, wiggling them furiously, as they propelled themselves along on the surface of the water.

It was all too dream-like and of unearthly beauty to leave to go downstairs to eat, so Anh Hai brought us our sandwiches up on deck and we ate as we sat in our chairs entranced with the lovely sea pictures. What a contrast this was to our dark green jungle trips!

Masses of clouds piled up like white towers on the horizon and were reflected in the calm, blue ocean. Everything was pale blue, shot through with delicate lavender and gleams of white, and even a canoe could have traversed the still waters without danger.

Our pilot used a compass and after several hours, the tip of low-lying Ly Son Island appeared straight ahead of us on the horizon. The island is made up of volcanic hills and is four miles long. Our pilot knew how to enter the channel between the coral reefs, but we could not get closer than 300 yards from shore, as the bottom of the lagoon was full of coral rocks.

These coral waters have a snow-white sandy bottom, with different colored coral masses under the water, making the blues of the water every shade from purple to ultra-marine, to peacock and robin's-egg blue, and there are streaks of tender green where the coral castles reach near the surface.

We anchored in crystal blue-green water, fifteen feet deep, and we could see schools of fish going by. We even fed rice to large blue fish, three feet long, that had yellow fins and stripes. It was a fisherman's paradise but we had no tackle. Fishing boats quickly came to our boat to see us and to sell us some of their catch. I never saw such beautiful fish! The most outstanding were parrot-fish, two feet long, with parrot-like "beaks" and colorings of blue, green and rose with a yellow scroll-pattern, clearly marked, on their heads! Some fish were white with splashes of pink, yellow and black. Many were yellow with black stripes and trailing black fins like chiffon.

Groups of Vietnamese children, almost naked and black from being in the sun, swam out on boards and came aboard to visit us. Scores of people were out on the flats of coral at low tide gathering sea snails, oysters, clams, crabs — and other edibles they could find from the sea.

We went in by our coracle tub to visit the island. The people are all fishermen and have small farms, too. They cannot grow rice here, so they plant corn, sweet potatoes and manioc root and live mostly on an abundant diet of sea food. They are friendly country people — somewhat different from the mainland Vietnamese. Their island dialect is hard to understand.

They were glad to see Gordon and our workers again and we had a large meeting that night outside of the home of one family who were very interested in the Gospel. The people here were so open-hearted that a number quickly accepted the Gospel message, came forward and prayed to God. We had a fine student preacher, Mr. Huk, from Bato, who had just finished his second year in Bible School and was appointed to work on this Ly Son Island. He would be moving here with his family and would be their pastor in just a few days' time.

We spent the next day visiting scores of bamboo houses up and down the one main road, four miles in length. It is lined with hedges of hibiscus and in this season, the flower-bells were glowing red by the thousands. There are no cars on the island but the people have many bicycles.

Hordes of staring children followed us everywhere, whooping and yelling, and stood many feet deep in front of us, whenever we stopped to rest and witness at someone's house. Older people, too, swamped our workers for medicines, clamoring and clawing for the simple remedies which they so badly needed.

But it was wonderful to see their openness of heart and we preached until we nearly dropped with fatigue.

This was my first visit to the islands of Cu Lao Cham and Ly Son.

On a later trip, towards the end of September, Gordon and I, Mrs. Thuan, the nurse evangelist, and Anh Hai, were back on the "Hy-Vong" to visit these islands again. Mr. and Mrs. Huk and family had already been moved to Ly Son and were having good success in sowing the seed and reaping a harvest for God. On this trip we now met with his good group of converts and visited in their homes. We were able to bring some bags of American

Relief supplies to the islanders — rice, beans, bulgar-wheat, corn-meal and some furniture for the Huk family.

The islanders gave us beautiful sea-shells of all shapes and sizes. Some were large Tritons, with the call of the ocean coming out of their rosy chambers. They also had beautiful pieces of coral for us — delicate lacy branches in pink, rose and yellow.

We were there over a week-end and on the Friday, Gordon and Nam, our pilot, took a very sick girl and some of her relatives, the twenty-two mile trip across to the mainland, to the government hospital at Quang Ngai.

As they returned to the island, the ocean was getting rough, with a north wind churning up the sea. When they anchored again they put out three Danforth anchors of varying sizes, one held by Manilla rope and two by coconut ropes. As long as the wind came from the north we felt safe behind the coral reef shelter.

But on that Friday night, the wind blew harder and harder and the boat pitched and rolled. We knew we were coming near the typhoon season, but they usually do not break until October.

On Saturday the rains came in torrents, the wind rose to startling gale force; and the sea was rising very high. The combers poured over the coral reef and we in the lagoon were rolling wildly in the trough of the waves. We must watch that our anchor ropes didn't get cut on the sharp, biting coral below us. We asked one of the islanders to stay on board to help us, as he was an expert diver. Using a mask over his nose and eyes, he made frequent trips below, following the anchor ropes to see if they were being chafed. Twice the coconut ropes broke and he had to retrieve the anchors and mend the ropes. How we wished we had steel cables for the anchors — around these sharp coral rocks!

We anxiously watched the wind swing around to the west. If it should turn to the south, it would become a typhoon and we'd be in grave danger for we would get the full force of wind and sea through a southern gap in the reefs. We were in the best shelter that there was on the island.

All Saturday night the boatmen and the diver watched our anchor ropes, for if they all gave way at once, we would be blown out to sea and would be like a chip in the storm.

Sunday morning dawned with hurricane winds and driving rain! Sure enough, the gale was coming now directly from the south, piling furious waves over the reef and through the gap straight at our tossing, rolling boat! We tried several times to swing the boat to face the wind and waves but the cross current was too strong and our anchor ropes snapped. Our boat must weigh twenty tons and it is fifty feet long with a deep keel. We just had to sit there struggling in the steep, violent gray-green waves, swelling to great heights, some washing along the deck. We would rise up on a huge green cliff, as if we were soaring on wings, for a moment rest poised upon the foaming crest and then fall, wallowing down into the seething valley.

Things in our cabin and anything loose below deck, rolled and plunged. Bilge water was slopping over the floor of the boat. Nam and the boatman, Tam, and the diver watched the anchor ropes continually. Gordon started the engine and took charge of the steering wheel, in case the anchor ropes all broke at once. We put on our life-belts now and Anh Hai was pumping out the bilge water by hand-pump as fast as he could.

I was with Gordon in the pilot house and we were pitched from side to side. Gordon had a hard time holding on to the steering wheel and I had to hang on to doors and cupboards with all my might for fear of being thrown across the pilot house and down the stair-well. The waves toppled on to the deck, hissing and seething.

By 5 P.M. Sunday afternoon the wind rose even stronger, screaming in our ears and tearing at our boat. We cried to God now for fear that we might lose our lovely boat. It was almost dark when Gordon said to me, "The only way to save the ship now is to beach it and we will go on shore now to direct it in."

The brave, little Vietnamese pilot, Nam, took over the wheel and Tam unleashed our coracle tub and I was to jump down into it on the lee side. I was really afraid to jump, as it bobbed like a cork on the huge, heavy hills of water. But Gordon cried, "Jump *now* or we'll be swamped under!" I saw a mountain of wave coming to engulf us, so I jumped and landed in the little basket and kept my face down. Gordon jumped after me and we rose high on the vast hill of water and came trembling down into the trough.

Tam, the Vietnamese, paddled us over the billows safely into shore.

Our workers, Mr. and Mrs. Huk and nurse, Mrs. Thuan, were down on their knees crying to God for us. "We thought you'd be drowned!" they cried, throwing their arms around us. A large crowd had gathered on the shore and had been watching us for a long time. The boat, back in the water, looked like a white butterfly in the dark, green-black, foaming billows.

All three anchor ropes broke now, so Nam, the pilot, pointed the brave little ship in toward the shore. Gordon and the fishermen on the shore, waved and guided Nam through a shallow channel. We all cried aloud to God to save the boat!

It came bumping over the coral rocks with each wave helping it along. The tide was now coming in and helped push the boat forward until it finally came to rest on the beach, tilted on its side. How we praised God that the boat was safe and seemingly undamaged.

We clambered aboard and brought bedding and food and the islanders helped carry our belongings in the rain and dark to a nearby new Christian's bamboo hut. We ate a little food and then fell asleep quite exhausted. The pilot brought everything off the ship, although this was not necessary, and we were too tired to notice that he piled a lot of it outside under the thatched roof entrance to the house, instead of putting it all inside the house.

About four in the morning, the old man of the house woke us to say that someone had come and stolen a lot of our stuff which had been left outside the door. A large aluminum water tank, that Nam had packed up with clothing and shoes, was gone and a large sack of other things was missing — two steel thermos bottles, my Vietnamese Bible, some study books, pots, pans and raincoats. The police came and made a list and said they would scour the island for the thief.

Dawn broke, with the sun shining, and the typhoon, which was called "Typhoon Babs" and which had done a lot of damage on the mainland, was all passed away! We went to the beach and it was a great joy to see our white boat, high and almost dry, and in no danger now. We could see no damage done to it and how we praised God for the deliverance. Nam, not yet a Christian, marveled over and over at the way God helped us through the tempest.

The islanders now told us that we must get the boat off by noon, when the tide would be full again and there would be waves to help lift it. The keel was deep in the sand, but as the water rose slowly by eleven o'clock, the fifty men helping to push, could rock the boat a bit, and it began to float. As the shallow waves came in, the crowd of men, heaved and yelled and the bow was finally pushed around a little. Nam ran the engine. The entry for the seawater which cools the engine was clogged up with sand, but Nam had to race the motor anyway, without the cooling water. Everyone pushed hard. Sand and water churned up and finally the boat began to inch slowly out. With great shouts and pushing, it at last floated free from the beach. But it was still in the shallow water and had to be pushed 100 yards, bumping over the coral, until it was in deep water and safe. Then we all thanked God with fervent hearts for His wonderful help in bringing the little ship back to life again.

The weather was clear now and we planned to leave next day. We had to get two of the twisted anchors straightened out in a little primitive forge in the village, and we threw away our broken ropes and bought a new one-inch coconut rope from the islanders. We preached some more to good crowds of people that day and evening. They were drawn closer to us now in sympathy, as we had gone through a storm such as they often experience here.

On Tuesday morning as we heaved anchor, Huk and a number of Christians came out to our boat by sampan to say good-by.

The sea was now a lovely, lustrous smooth blue again and we sat out on deck enjoying the whole calm twelve-hour trip home.

At dark we chugged up the Da Nang River with the colored lights of the town like flames down in the black water, undulating gently on slight ripples.

We found that the rudder post had been damaged slightly at the socket from bumping on the coral but this was soon fixed. We bought new steel cables for our anchors and everything was ship-shape again.

The police also found most of our things on the island and later on, Mr. Huk returned them to us.

Two fishermen in their little sailboat saw some books floating on the water. One of the fishermen knew that one of the books was the Word of God — my Vietnamese Bible! He cried, "God has shown His power to me! Mr. and Mrs. Huk couldn't find this Book, and the police couldn't find it. No one could find it, but God brought it to me out on these waves! So now I will believe on God."

He was a man 31 years of age. He came back and returned my other four note-books to Huk, but he said, "I won't give you the Bible, for God has given it to me. I can read these words." He put the Bible on a little rack over the fire to dry out page by page. He heard God speaking to him through the Book and he went to Mr. Huk and said he couldn't reject God's Word. He accepted Christ and began meeting with the other Christians regularly.

Some months later he went over to Quang Ngai by sailboat and then came by bus to Da Nang and to our house, to tell us all about it, and his happy faith in Christ. He is a leading elder in the Ly Son Island church today, reading the precious Word and going on with God.

There was much eye disease on the island and as we next visited there, Evangelist Huk lined up all of these eye patients. Dr. Herb Billman was flown in from Da Nang by a small American military plane and for several hours he, with another of our student-workers, Mr. Toi, who was now Dr. Billman's valuable medical assistant, examined the eyes and selected those who should come to Da Nang for eye operations. There were eighty patients in all.

We had them brought to Da Nang by the "Hy-Vong" in several trips and Dr. Billman operated on them. They were able to stay in a big room, kindly lent to us by the City Administration, while the doctor treated them for several weeks. Then the boat took them back to Ly Son Island again.

This made a great impression on the islanders, causing them to be more friendly than ever to us.

Today a nice church has been built there with the Christians all helping in the building of it. It was finished by Christmas, 1963, and shortly afterward we went there to help dedicate it.

Also four Vietnamese men have recently accepted Christ on the Cu Lao Cham Island. We believe that God will fan this little spark into a big flame until the people of this island will turn to Christ and spirituality will take the place of deadness in their hearts.

▶ 23 ◀

Orphans!

CHILDREN, WITH FATHERS shot before their eyes! Boys and girls bereft of loved parents and left to the mercy of unprincipled relatives. The aftermath of war — always the suffering children, the needy ones.

What should we do about it? What would you have done? What did Jesus do?

"When mothers of Salem brought their children to Jesus, the stern disciples drove them back and bade them all depart; but Jesus saw them ere they fled, and sweetly smiled and kindly said, 'Suffer little children to come unto Me, for I will receive them and fold them to My bosom; I'll be a Shepherd to these lambs, O drive them not away; for, if their hearts to Me they give, they shall with Me in glory live; suffer little children to come unto Me.' How kind was our Saviour to bid these children welcome! — But there are many thousands who have never learned His name; the Bible they have never read; they know not that the Saviour said, 'Suffer little children to come unto Me.'"

There were the five Hiep children whose father was buried alive!

There was Cong, the wild, wolf-like street urchin, a crippled beggar, homeless.

There were three boys from Ankhe, that preacher Giang brought to us, whose father had been shot and their little mother left with five other children.

There was Minh, a beautiful, fair child, half-French and Vietnamese, nearly starved, with distended stomach, whom our native preacher at Camphu brought back to life.

196

There were many tribal children, slaves, illiterate, with hopeless futures, two especially, Tieu and Ca Rop.

We began by taking in thirty-three children in July, 1962, housing them in our Bible School dormitories during the summer vacation months.

After all our years, another new horizon widened out with unlimited possibilities! Here was another big challenge to faith — a challenge we knew our faithful prayer-helpers in the homelands would eagerly accept.

Step by step God led us.

A representative of the Christian Children's Fund Inc., having heard of the Hiep children, visited us, asking if C.C.F. could take on their support. He informed us that this great Organization which is helping over 45,000 needy children around the world, would be in a position to sponsor as many children, up to two hundred to begin with, that we could bring in.

They would give each child a sponsor who would send a small amount for food each month until the child was eighteen years old. In this way, our W.E.C. Children's Home became affiliated with the Christian Children's Fund, Incorporated.

Gordon and Mr. Nhut asked the Mayor of Da Nang for a site for the home at the foot of a mountain on the My Khe beach several miles from town. The Mayor replied, "That's too far! I'll give you some city lots right across on the main beach of My Khe nearby." On June 6, 1962, the authorization was received for twelve lots, measuring 130 by 65 yards in all.

Taking the plans with us, we were amazed to see that our site was on raised, practically level ground and probably was the most magnificent place in the whole area. It had a priceless view of the surrounding horizon in every direction — blue and purple mountains to the west and north and there, to the east, a few yards away is the wide, soft, sandy beach, lapped by the clear turquoise-blue waters of the South China Sea. Twenty miles away in the distance is the Cu Lao Cham Island, azure blue on fine days.

All the front of our property is planted with hundreds of the long-leaf pine trees, called filao, adding greatly to the beauty of the place. The almost empty beach stretches south for hundreds

Top: Orphans, three Vietnamese superintendents and teachers, and the Smiths.

Left: Christmas day for the orphans meant a visit with the Marines.

Below: Three little girls and their dolls (gifts of the U.S. Marines, Christmas Day, 1963); a Polaroid shot of Cong, the wild orphan from the streets of Da Nang.

Top: Orphans at My Khe playing with beach ball, gift from America.
Right: Playing on the slide donated by U. S. Special Forces.
Below: U. S. Marines level the orphanage beach site.

of miles with nothing but a few fishing villages, with their sail-boats drawn up and nets hung out to dry.

It was with deep thankfulness that we met and dedicated this most beautiful, healthful, convenient spot, in which to bring up little children. We could not want any greater proof of God's favor toward this new project.

Under the care of a splendid Christian Vietnamese man and his wife, and a retired Vietnamese pastor, the children have school classes each day and much instruction in the Bible, memorizing Bible verses, the catechism, singing hymns and praying. Soon each little child had accepted Christ as his or her Saviour. They are very good, obedient, gentle children, easy to train in nice manners.

One night, when Gordon was away on a trip, three American sergeants came to our house asking us to take in a wild Vietnamese crippled beggar, called Cong, who was running the streets in an awful state of filth and need. Mr. Lich went with the three soldiers in their car and found the boy, twelve years old, sleeping out on one of the benches by the Da Nang River. They carried him in their arms into the car and to our Bible School building, with the boy kicking and fighting. The sergeants had seen this waif here in Da Nang for three months in the same dirty rags and sleeping by the river and they often took pity on him and fed him. He would stand at their hotel dining room window every day. As they brought him to us, they said, "We can't take it any more. He watches every mouthful we eat."

Pamela Brady, the nurse, came and between her and Mr. Lich, they cut off his dirty rags, with him fighting and howling like a wild animal all the time. We brought towels and a big aluminum wash basin full of warm water and Pam bathed him with disinfect-ant and soap, as the others held his arms, legs and mouth. He tried hard to bite them. One of his arms is withered and he has a club hand. This he had hidden in his rag shirt and fought, kicked and bit, determined not to let anyone see it. The unlettered Vietna-mese people tell anyone who is crippled that he has a devil. Cong's legs are also misshapen and he is a little lame. He had some bad sores on his legs.

The American soldiers went downtown while he was getting

bathed and bought him a pair of nice blue pajamas; cowboy jeans and a red plaid shirt and belt.

Pam and Mr. Lich got him into the pajamas with his withered arm hidden and Pam bandaged up his sores. They carried him to one of the beds made up for an orphan, with a clean mat, pillow and mosquito net. All of this took from 8:30 to 11 P.M. as Cong put up such a fight. He still roared and wept loudly. Pam gave him an injection to make him sleep, but he hit out at us with his one good hand until 12 P.M. Mr. Lich sat by him, holding him all the time, sometimes in his arms like a baby. Pam fanned him. Finally he slept and we could all get to bed.

Next morning he was sullen and ugly and refused to eat anything. He kept trying to get away but we closed up the gates. The American sergeants would be coming back to see him. They wanted to support him, while they were here in Viet Nam, and were eager for us to make a home for him. But he was wild to get back to his begging as different Americans had given him candy, gum, pop and money for the cinemas. He didn't want to live inside a house. From Quang Ngai, and an orphan, he had been living outside like a dog for years. What a sad case! Our students and helpers said they had often seen him downtown and they told us there were more like him in this city.

It took all our morning to hold him and to try to pacify him. Once he did get away from us, climbing a fence, but Dam, our gardener, ran after him and carried him back. He threw himself on the ground in his nice new clothes, tore off all his bandages and pitched handfuls of dirt and stones at us, and bit the superintendent's hand. He was truly like a wild animal.

Then the three big, tall American soldiers came with their soft, kind Southern talk and he quieted down for them. They took Polaroid photos of him and then showed him his face so sad and swollen with crying. They put the photos into plastic folders taken from their wallets and placed these in the pocket of his new pajamas. One of the kind Americans went downtown and bought pop and a bowl of rice and chicken for him. Mr. Lich sat by him encouraging him to eat. This was the first he had eaten since he came to us. Our little monkey played around him and Cong couldn't help but like the comical little pet. The soldiers took photos of the monkey, too, and gave one to Cong and he was pleased.

But when the American men left he screamed and howled again, and threw dust and stones. Dam tried to carry him into a room but Cong hit him, and ran out of our gate and down the road yelling. A car full of Vietnamese people stopped and asked him what was the matter? He said we were stealing him, beating him on the head, and trying to throw him down into the sewer. We had to explain that this was not the truth. Chi Nga and Dam carried Cong back to our house again. We made a bed for him, with a mat, out on our front veranda and he finally ate up the rest of his chicken and rice there, and some meat and fried potatoes I gave him. He didn't want to be near the other children as he was ashamed of his crippled arm and legs. He slept out on the veranda mat.

When the three American soldiers left for the States soon after this, Cong gradually settled down with us. One day I found out that he could read and write and I gave him some little lessons and was surprised at his quickness in arithmetic and reading.

One and a-half years of living here in our mission compound has made a tremendous change in Cong. Now he goes to a Da Nang school regularly, after being thrown out of the first two. He sings lustily in church with his loud, raucous voice, from his own hymn-book, has his own Bible and has already earnestly prayed.

He still refuses to go to the Orphange to live, as he is still too ashamed of his poor arm and club hand. Also we dare not put him there yet for fear he might upset the good discipline of the other children. He eats here with the Bible School students and plays with all of their children and is happy and content. What a changed boy he is today!

He could rehabilitate his hand if he would work on the fingers and muscles, but he refuses to do this yet. Pamela Brady would like to soak his arm and hand and work with him on the exercises, and we think he may allow her to do so soon.

> "I dare not slight the stranger at my gate —
> Threadbare of garb, and sorrowful of lot,
> Lest it be Christ that stands, and goes His way,
> Because I, all unworthy, knew Him not."

When the Bible School opened again on September 1, 1962, and the students came crowding in to their dormitories, some Vietnamese friends kindly loaned us, for the orphans, their summer home of three rooms, on the ocean beach, right next to our own new Orphanage property. The children and their superintendents lived temporarily in this place until we could get the funds to construct our first building.

The first work we did on our Orphanage site was to dig a small well for a fresh water supply and we built a temporary kitchen out of bamboo and thatch grass.

American officers and men were pouring in to Viet Nam now in an advisory capacity to the Vietnamese army, and there were about 1,000 Americans now stationed in Da Nang alone. They were made up of Army, Navy, Air Force, Marines, Special Forces, and Signal Corps.

Some of them, hearing of our Orphanage, wanted to help give the children a fine Christmas, and the Chaplains cooperated with us in a wonderful way. There is nothing like little children to touch the hearts of the men in the armed forces, many of whom are reminded of their own little ones back home.

So the orphans' first Christmas was a wonderful time! The children put on their own little program for us missionaries on December 22. Their house was all trimmed and they had a nice Christmas tree. Their teachers had trained them well in songs, recitations and drills. They were dressed in their new uniforms given to them by the Marines — blue pants or skirts with white shirts or blouses, with new socks and sandals. Their hair was slicked down and their faces scrubbed and shining. Playing on the sandy beach had turned all of them a deep brown and they were the picture of health.

Then we gave them their presents, mostly gifts from the Americans. These were the first toys they had ever owned. The little children — age from 4 to 12 — clasped their dolls, cars, puzzles, toy animals and candy in their arms, speechless with joy! The Mennonite Central Committee from America also sent a parcel for each child, each with its little sticker, "In the Name of Christ." So now the children each owned his first towel and sweater. The house was soon full of whoops and laughter, buzzing noises and whistles

— all so much fun! Cong, too, had his share in all of this with the others.

We were still in the midst of these shouts of glee when we heard the rumbling of a big motor outside. It was the U.S. Marines arriving with a bulldozer on a long, low carrier, to level off our new Orphanage site. Before we could start building, there would have to be about a thousand yards of sand dunes pushed and leveled.

It was a misty, rainy day but the bulldozer soon crawled off sideways from the truck and climbed to the high level of the property and started to work at once. A Marine engineer captain and the Protestant chaplain came along to see that everything went well. Soon the kiddies were staring wide-eyed, as the tall Americans worked all that day and the next to prepare a place for their future home.

Another military group, called M.A.A.G. (United States Military Advisors Group) also helped in our orphans' Christmas, besides giving offerings of money each month for the orphans. For some weeks at their PX (Commissary Store) they had placed large cartons, one for our orphans and the other for the Catholic orphans in town, with a big notice covered with photos of the children, asking for donations of soap, tooth brushes, wash cloths, candies, etc. So on the afternoon of December 23, a lovely party was prepared especially for our children. The children of the Catholic Orphanage would have their party on Christmas day.

To bring our children across from their beach-site home to the enlisted men's mess, meant having trucks bring them to the river. Then, since the big bridge across the river had been destroyed in the recent typhoon and flood, they had to get into small plastic assault motor-boats and they were whisked through choppy waves (the wind was high and some of us got splashed) to be loaded into another big bus for the drive to the party. The children were met at the door by a number of officers and men, who took charge of them, showed them the American Christmas tree lit up like a glowing jewel, with a pile of intriguing plastic bags filled with good things underneath the branches; past the huge frosted cake with, "Welcome Children" written across it; then to seat them, four at a table, for a feast of ice-cream and cake. They had never tasted such delicious food in their lives!

Before the presents were given out, the children sang some of their songs and did interesting drills for their hosts. They were pretty full of cake and ice-cream, candy and pop, and oranges, but they managed to carry it out well. Their discipline was a joy to behold.

Then one of the officers made a speech and the plastic bundles of things from the PX and toys, each with the name of a child on it, were handed to them.

One American officer was so deeply touched that he went to Gordon saying, "How can I help these kiddies? I feel I should do something for them." Gordon replied that since they now had clothes and toys, any gift would be put toward a house for them to live in, of their very own. So the officer promptly wrote out a check for one hundred dollars and gave it to Gordon toward the first house on the Orphange site.

Back into the bus again, and across the river, the children looked almost overwhelmed at all the marvelous things and good times they were having. Into another large truck again, and they were taken to their three-room house, one room of which was a bedroom for them all. They slept together on planks on the floor until the day when we could give them each separate beds of their own.

The Marines invited the orphans to Christmas dinner on December 25.

Two Marine trucks went over on a ferry to bring the children back to the Marine Air Base in Da Nang. Each child was met by a "father" who not only took charge of his child, but had bought a present for him or her. They showed the children around one of the many big helicopters which go out on missions every day to carry Vietnamese troops into battle and bring back the wounded.

In the mess hall, the children put on part of their program of drills and songs, then the group of Marines took them outside to play with their new toys. Big burly men tenderly carried the little orphan girls in their arms and they told us they were thinking of their own little girls back home.

Then at 4 o'clock the call to Christmas dinner came. The "fathers" took their children by the hand along the "chow line," helping to heap up their plates with turkey, ham, vegetables and all kinds of wonderful food flown all the way from America. This was a touching sight to see these men, who are in constant danger over the jungles of Viet Nam, graciously sharing their bountiful Christmas dinner with kiddies who do not yet know how to use a knife and fork. Used to chopsticks, the children had to have their food cut up in small pieces for them and they ate with spoons. There was mince pie, Christmas cake, great blobs of green ice-cream, apples and oranges from California, nuts and candies, cool drinks, everything to make the most delicious dinner to be found anywhere in the world.

The orphans never had such joy in all their lives. They had just known starvation, abuse, slavery; some had seen their parents murdered by the Communists before their eyes. Not only were the children invited, but our three Vietnamese workers who are in charge of them, and Gordon and I, also enjoyed it to the full. But that was not all . . .

The Commanding Officer and the Chaplain then presented us with a sum of money the men had contributed for the Orphanage building fund amounting to eight hundred dollars! Then they gave us another hundred dollars especially to purchase more clothing for the children.

Gordon bought some cheap tin suitcases for each child and when he drove up to the orphans' house next day with a car-load of these tinny-looking valises, the children came running out, shouting, "Hallelujah, Praise the Lord!" Their little hearts were overflowing with thanks and praise. Now they can keep their own clothes and toys together, for up to that time, they had no furniture except a couple of long tables and some benches.

After all this magnificent effort on the part of the American Forces in Da Nang for our orphans, it is difficult to find words to adequately express our thanks for all they did. Our hearts were deeply touched with their sacrifices and generosity. We rejoiced to know that quite a number of the men really loved the Lord. During the past months we had shown our movies of our work several times to the various military groups, especially the film made by Dave and Gwen Cornell, "Jungle Beach-heads." The

men also bought many of our books on our work in Viet Nam —
Gongs in the Night and *Farther Into the Night.*

Their gifts, along with that of another wonderful fellow-worker
in America, meant that we could now begin construction on the
first two buildings, and we began these at once.

We planned to erect one big double-story dormitory, six other
buildings and a chapel, to hold at least 300 needy children, waiting to be brought in. Our first house was finished by March,
and was big enough to permit our 34 children to live in it, with
a room for the Superintendent and his wife. Gifts also came in to
provide nice double-decker beds for the children.

All the rooms look out over the grove of trees and sand to
the sea. Some days, blue skies sweep over a quiet, sparkling ocean
with the latteen sailing-boats flitting by. Other days the water
is gray-green with black clouds overhead and gales whipping
up the waves until they can see —

"the wild white horses play,
champ and chafe and toss in the spray."

There is the lovely smell of the sea and they can hear its soft
sighs and murmurs, or its loud bellows and deep roars. Breezes
come in their bedroom windows straight off the water.

The eastern sky opens in flower colors on many mornings and
the full moon lavishes its white light over the ocean. It is an
earthly paradise.

As we compare the photos we took of the children a year and
a-half ago, with the children today, we are amazed. They are now
so fat, brown and healthy. There has been hardly any sickness
among them. They eat big pots of rice mixed with the especially
prepared Bulgar-wheat from America, and lots of fish from the
sea.

Their second building is a temporary kitchen and dining room,
that can be added to, to provide larger space for these facilities.

Recently a large well, 12 x 12 feet, has been dug to give plenty
of fresh water in the dry season. It is quite shallow and only one
hundred feet from the sea-shore, but the water is sweet. A water
tower has also been built.

Work is almost finished now on the much needed building with
toilets and bathing facilities. We have thirty more children

WAGGONER CHRISTIAN CHURCH

screened and ready to be brought in as soon as another dormitory is erected.

The children have strict discipline and are very obedient. They are learning deep lessons from God's Word and they love to sing choruses and many of the well-known Action Songs. Already two of the older children testify that God has called them to enter our Bible School when they finish their training at the Orphanage at eighteen years of age, and they want to study to be workers for the Lord here in Viet Nam.

The children turn their work hours into play — clearing up the yards, gathering sticks and filao needles for fire, sweeping out their rooms. We have taught them how to play baseball and volley ball and now the Special Forces have donated some fine playground equipment — swings, slides and teeter-totters. We must also build a proper school-building with vocational-training facilities.

The W.E.C. Children's Home is a "promised land" to these children. "Now we are all happy!" they cry. What a joyous place it will be when there are three hundred rescued children brought here to Jesus, many of whom will prepare to work for Him in full-time service in days to come.

▶ 24 ◀
Battles

THE SECOND BATTLE OF Tra Bong was more fierce than the first. Six hundred Communist guerillas attacked. It was two years since they first tried to take this frontier village, with our chapel only a few feet away from the fort. The chapel was badly damaged then and our workers, the Cuu family and Quang, the Cua preacher, miraculously escaped by hiding in a fox-hole nearby.

Now the Communists came in greater force and the battle raged for three days. Many were killed on both sides. Once again the Lord miraculously cared for our dear Vietnamese preacher and his wife, Mr. and Mrs. Cuu, and their family of two beautiful little girls and baby boy. Two days after the battle, Cuu and Quang came in to Da Nang, bedraggled and exhausted, and told us the news. This is Cuu's story:

"At midnight the Communists overran Tra Bong. We were all sleeping. Quang was across the river with his family and the Communists attacked there, too. Mortar shells were coming from the surrounding hills and landing all around us. Bullets spattered like rain. The six outlying forts were also attacked. As the bullets came through the mud walls of the chapel, we all lay flat on the ground. Many were crying out and being killed and the ground shook with the explosions.

"At eight A.M. the Communists entered the chapel and ordered us to open up all the doors and windows and go outside. They said they had killed all the government troops. My wife said to them, 'We are very frightened!' One Communist, after finding out that we were preachers, said, 'Lie down or you'll get killed!'

As he was talking to us, a government soldier came up and shot him in the leg. He called out, 'Oh, heaven, I am dying!' Communist soldiers came and carried him away. Another Communist came into the chapel and also told us to stay on the ground. As he went out the door, he was shot and killed. We were much afraid and saw it was too dangerous to stay there. We crawled slowly along the ground toward the market place nearby and found a shallow trough to lie in.

"We stayed in that ditch for three days and two nights with little to eat or drink. Some people brought us some sweet potatoes. Fighting was going on all around us. Many were dying and the stench of dead bodies was awful. The flies and ants were everywhere. People were crushed, broken and in terror. Two light bombers of the Viet Nam Air Force came and bombed in the mountains all day Friday and Saturday. Twelve big American helicopters arrived, bringing in government troops. At times my heart seemed to stop beating and my hands and feet had no feeling. I could not speak. My wife cried and every few minutes we would have to press the baby's head down to the ground for fear of flying bullets.

"We asked the Communists to let us go out of the town, but they refused. They said, 'We're going to take you up into the mountains with us, and we're also going to take this whole village of Tra Bong.' But later on, during the last of the battle, we were able to crawl farther away and then walk and run, carrying the three children, and made a roundabout trip to the home of a Christian. We were almost dead from exhaustion.

"Finally, the Communists were pushed back and on Sunday we could return to the chapel. We were afraid to go to sleep because the Communists said they would be back again. But they did not come.

"The chapel is half destroyed. The Administrator says we must pull it down now in order to have all the space around the fort free. We must find another site and build a new chapel now. Four of our Christians were taken by the Communists."

This was the end of Cuu's story. Long, one of our first Cua Christians, who has had one year in our Bible School, but who is at present called into the Viet Nam Army, told his story:

"With nine others, I was caught by the Communists when they attacked Tra Bong. Our hands were tied behind our backs and we were taken two days' walk into the mountains. But I found that I could finally untie the rope binding my hands, so when the time came, I did so. Then I untied the man in front of me, secretly, and he and all the others, did the same for the man in front of each of them, until all of us nine prisoners were free. Then we killed the two Communists and we all got back home safely."

Cuu and Quang were dead-tired and ill from the strain, but they were anxious to get back to Tra Bong, because Quang said there were several new Cua tribesmen who wanted to believe on Christ.

A few months after this, Gordon and I, Mr. Nhut and the Bible-evangelistic car with its team of three fine Vietnamese preachers, went out to dedicate the newly rebuilt chapel at Tra Bong, on a new site, one mile away from its former place. We had a great time of fellowship with these workers and all the faithful group of Christians there. Today there is an airfield on the area where our former chapel and the market was. A group of fourteen men of American Special Forces moved in and there is now a large military camp here and all is quiet at present in Tra Bong area.

At about the same time, Mr. and Mrs. Roy Spraggett from Cam Phu, among the Baru tribespeople, just south of the 17th Parallel, wrote:

"Last night our dear brother in the Lord, Yong (the Baru Christian tribes-worker), was taken by the Communists. A large band of them came into his village late at night, bound him, and held a meeting of Communist propaganda with the rest of the village. They took no one else, but led Yong away, bound, into the mountains. They broke down the protecting fence around the village and scattered Communist leaflets around the place.

"It would be hard for us to express the love and admiration we have for this dear Baru brother. He has faithfully served the Lord with a full heart since we have known him here at Cam Phu and have worked with him."

Later we found out through some Baru who escaped over the border from the Communists, that Yong was imprisoned in a tiny

Communist cell across the 17th Parallel border, with only two bowls of rice a day, and was being let out from his dungeon only once a day. He may not be alive now.

The other Baru Christian worker at Cam Phu, Oai, was also taken away by the Communists and we hear that he has been shot. These first Baru Christians of Cam Phu now wear the martyr's Crown of Life.

Since then, still another Baru who loved the Lord, Tenon, has been taken away by the Communists! His little wife, with her baby, ran after him, pleading with the Communists to let her husband go, but they held a gun to her head and told her they would shoot her if she didn't go back to her hut.

All of this persecution of the Christians makes the other Baru tribespeople today very wary. Many would like to turn to Christ but they fear that by doing so they might be taken by the Communists as were Yong, Oai and Tenon.

The Communists also attacked Ba An, our new station on the road into Bato. They tied up our preacher there, Mr. Hoc, and would have taken him back into the hills, but in the confusion of the battle, God helped Hoc to loosen his bonds and get away.

The Communists ordered Mrs. Thuan, the nurse who is now working at Ba An, to give up all the medicines she had to them. If she had not done so, they would have killed her.

The Trebilcos living at Bato are often within the sound of guns. When the big 155 m/m artillery guns go off from the fort at Bato, the windows of their little house are shaken and there is now hardly any putty left on them. The Treblicos make frequent trips the forty miles into Quang Ngai, taking wounded soldiers to the hospital there. God has kept them from being molested.

It is only an hour's trip by plane across the mountains from Da Nang to Kontum where Stanley, Ginny and their new baby, Kenny, were now working. It takes twelve hours to go by road. Leaving the scorching heat of Da Nang, I was lonely with Gordon staying behind, but he couldn't go on this trip to Kontum with me at this time.

The plane headed into the mountains and it began to get cloudy and cold. We bounced badly, and after an hour, I looked out

Mr. Nhut prays for sick child of Yong, the Baru Christian who was later captured by the communists and is probably dead now.

Baru Christian worker at Cam Phu. Oai was taken by the communists and his fate is unknown.

A Jeh resettlement village, protected by sharpened bamboo fences from communist invasion. It has repulsed several attacks.

the window expecting to see Kontum below, but there was no sign of the town — just rugged mountains which seemed so close. Stan and Ginny told me later that they heard our plane passing over Kontum through the clouds and pelting rain. They began to worry about how we'd get down as the Vietnamese operator at Kontum who ran the radio beam was out to lunch!

But at last they saw our plane skimming back, low over the town and we landed safely. My legs were weak under me as I got out of the plane, for we'd been lost in the storm for quite a time among the high, dangerous mountains, and with no radio beam, but the Vietnamese pilot was an ace to finally bring us in safely.

How good it was to see our dear children and our new little grandson, Kenny!

That evening we went out to the officers' quarters of the U. S. Advisory Group, M.A.A.G., and they all hailed baby Kenny with joy, each officer taking him in turn and playing with him. He reminded them of their own children back in America. Colonel T., the officer in Command of M.A.A.G., invited us to return on Saturday night for a celebration in honor of Major S., who would be promoted to Lt. Colonel.

Early next morning, we packed up to go the thirty miles north to our station of Dak To among the Sedang tribe. Gordon had already hauled our house-trailer from Da Nang up to this place and had parked it under a tree some months previously. Stan and Ginny were camping in it frequently as they were beginning to reach these Sedang tribal villages out from Dak To.

On the way, we passed places in the road that had been mined by the Communists just several days before. A number of Vietnamese soldiers had been killed and an American Major just escaped with his life.

We enjoyed camping in the nice trailer. But we could hear the distant rumble of heavy guns firing towards the border of Laos, as a big battle was going on at that time. Stan had dug a deep hole in the ground for us to jump into in case they turned the guns our way! It was muddy and liable to have huge beetles and bugs in it, so I dreaded the thought of getting down into it. But we committed ourselves to God and His words to us in Psalm

121 were: "The Lord is thy Keeper: the Lord shall keep thee from all evil. The Lord shall preserve thy going out and thy coming in." All was peaceful — just the pitter-patter of the cool rain on the trailer roof all night.

Next morning, we visited groups of Sedang tribespeople. As I told the flannelgraph stories in Vietnamese, Stanley translated into the Sedang language and my heart was greatly touched as I heard him talking Sedang fluently now. He had spent all of his childhood out here in Viet Nam, as we lived at Banmethuot, among the Raday tribespeople, and he speaks the Raday language. Now he is back in Viet Nam, speaking Vietnamese and this Sedang tribal language. What a joy to have one of our own sons, with his lovely wife, Ginny, and dear baby, Kenneth, ready now to open up this great Sedang tribe to the Gospel.

We also spent hours playing some gospel recordings in the Sedang and Rongao languages to the scores of tribespeople who stood around our trailer. Stan used one of the small $3.00 Gospel Recording phonographs which had to be turned by hand.

Back in Kontum again, we went to the American officers' promotion celebration on the Saturday night. There were 100 American officers and men at the M.A.A.G. there. They had an outside barbecue feast, eating tender steaks flown all the way from America.

Next morning while Stan, Ginny and I were at breakfast, we heard many helicopters buzzing over our house and we wondered where the battle was. Then we had our Vietnamese chapel service in Stan and Ginny's house. At 10:30, just as we were about to hold the meeting in English for some of the Protestant American officers who met each Sunday, we heard terrible news!

The first helicopter to go out that morning had been shot down by the Communists. Colonel T., the Head Commander of the Kontum M.A.A.G. group, who had played with our Kenny a few nights before and with whom we ate steak on the Saturday night, had been killed! The Communist bullets had hit the gas tank and it exploded. A Vietnamese Captain, whom we had also met at the party the night before, was instantly burned to death. Also the American Crew Chief of the helicopter was carbonized.

Colonel S., whose promotion we had celebrated the night be-

fore, was in the second helicopter and he saw the first one go
down in red balls of fire. He hovered down to forty feet, but
could see only a burned patch of ground and thought the helicopter had disintegrated. He dared not land for the place, no
doubt, was swarming with Communists and helicopters are extremely vulnerable. So they quickly whirred back to Kontum
and flew out squads of helicopters with a large band of Vietnamese soldiers into the area to hunt for the crashed helicopter men.
But by evening, the soldiers had not yet made contact with the
Communist guerillas or yet come to the place of the crash!

At dusk, Colonel S. flew back over the scene and a few miles
from it, he was hailed by one of the American majors of the
destroyed helicopter, waving a handkerchief down by the river.
The colonel dropped down and put the major in his place in the
helicopter. The colonel then waited in the river until another
helicopter came and lifted him out. It was growing dark but they
could see, right near the place of crash, another of the Americans
running around like a crazy man, below them. He wouldn't respond to their calls, but quickly ran and hid himself in the woods,
so they had to leave him that night.

Next morning, Monday, they found this poor man lying face
down in the river. The Communists had stripped him and shot
him through the head. His hands had been burned off in the
crash and he had awful face wounds. The pain had driven him
insane. He was the front gunner of the helicopter.

The rescued major told how when the burning helicopter
crashed, the front bubble had bounced off into the woods. The
two American pilots, one of them this major, were thrown right
through the plexiglass bubble. One pilot still had the seat strapped
around him and was dead. It was a miracle that the major survived. He was thrown ten feet away, and his back and shoulders
were badly hurt, but he gradually regained consciousness. He
found Colonel T. still alive in a piece of the plane, but his legs
were wedged between seats and were terribly crushed. The major
tried to pull him out but he couldn't, alone, with his hurt back.
He tried to help the gunner, and get him to go down the river
with him, but the gunner was in such frightful agony with his
hands burnt off and his face wounded that the major could do

nothing with him. The major thought he might find a tribal village along the river where he could get help and he had gone a mile or so when Colonel S. in the helicopter found him.

A second Vietnamese captain had been thrown from the helicopter about sixty feet into the woods and he lay hidden there with a broken leg. Some time later when he came out of his faint, he heard the Communists return and shoot Colonel T. five times until he died. The Americans in the rescue helicopters found the Vietnamese captain next morning, as he was still hidden in the bushes, and they got him back safely to camp. Four American top officers and one Vietnamese captain had been killed in the crash.

That same Monday morning a terrible tragedy occurred at the Kontum airport. A plane carrying 29 Vietnamese parachutists had an engine catch on fire on the takeoff. It circled and tried to land, but crashed on the runway and caught fire. The American co-pilot was killed, the Vietnamese pilot and twenty-four Vietnamese parachutists were burned to death. Only three paratroopers survived. Stan went down and saw the terrible wreckage, all twisted and charred.

At 4:30 that afternoon, we were told to go out to the airport if we wanted to see the last salute to the dead who were being shipped to Saigon. The bodies of the five Americans would be embalmed in Saigon and flown to their sad homes in America.

Stanley, Ginny and I drove out there. All the military and civilian officials in town were there — officers, troops and a band playing solemn music. Tanks lined the runway. Colonel S. was now taking Colonel T.'s place as Commander of the M.A.A.G. and he was deeply moved. The big C-123 cargo plane arrived from Saigon, circled, dipped in a salute, and landed. The great ramp in the rear swung down . . .

Then came five trucks slowly down the road, trimmed in flower-wreaths, each carrying the body of an American on a stretcher, covered with a golden Vietnamese flag with its three red stripes. One by one, the stretchers with their crumpled bodies were taken into the plane's huge maw — five Americans and one Vietnamese officer.

This was followed by the long cortege of twenty-five ambulance jeeps, each carrying the body of a paratrooper killed that morning. There had been no time to obtain flags, so they were just shielded with pieces of brown plastic sheets, commandeered a few minutes before from the soldiers lining the field. The bodies were all placed inside the big plane. The band played sorrowful music continually and the taps were sounded. Then the plane took off into the dusk for Saigon.

This is just one example of how American men are giving their lives out here in this battle for freedom from the Communists. One hundred and fifty Americans had died already, as of the end of 1963.

If the thousands of Americans had not come in to help train the Vietnamese, the country would, months ago, have fallen to the Communists.

A nice chapel has now been built in Kontum for the evangelists, Mr. and Mrs. Kinh and their family. Stan, Ginny and Kenny now are living continually in the trailer and a shack, at Dak To, while their new brick house, up on wooden posts, is being built there on the side of the road in this Sedang tribal center.

Three fine chapels have been built at Dak Psi, Dak Sut and Dak Pek, and Vietnamese evangelists are the missionaries to the tribes in these centers. Thuong is at Dak Pek among the Jeh there, learning this tribal language. An and his wife are now at Dak Sut, also learning the Jeh language. Tuu and his wife and family, formerly at Dak Sut, are back in Bible School for this year but will return to Dak Sut when school closes, as Tuu speaks the Jeh language quite well now. Mr. Thanh and his family are carrying on well at Dak Psi.

We are able to build many of these chapels today through the kind offer of the Native Church Crusade of Dallas, Texas, who send us $250.00 toward the finishing of each church that the native Christians may have begun but are unable to complete. This is a great encouragement to the churches who are struggling through all the difficulties of war. So much of their time is taken up with building fortifications and patrolling. How grateful we are for the sacrifice of many of God's people who are supporting this magnificent effort.

We now have twenty-five chapels in our District and forty-four national evangelists and workers and seventeen foreign missionaries. John Haywood and Brian Wilde arrived from England in 1963 to join our missionary group.

Our missionaries and national workers have great courage and faith to live in these lonely, isolated, dangerous places in these days of war. These servants of God are strong to see their duty to bring the story of Christ to these poor Jeh, Sedang, Hrey, Cua, Baru and all the other tribes and far-back Vietnamese. They stand on Psalms 90 and 91 which are great Psalms for them in these war years.

▶ 25 ◀

The Hreys Turn to Christ

THE STRATEGIC HAMLET PROGRAM has brought eight million people in Viet Nam into fortified villages. In many tribal areas this has meant that thousands of these mountain people have become accessible to the Gospel almost overnight. We are simply unable to take advantage of all these opportunities for lack of missionaries.

One area, especially, shows what can be accomplished when the foreign missionary and national worker cooperate in an intense effort in evangelism and medical help to these needy and bewildered throngs. They have been uprooted from their homes back in the jungle mountains and have been brought in to the roadsides and thrown together in large groups. Dr. Stuart Harverson, together with Dinh Nai, our trained Hrey preacher, have seen 700 of these resettled Hrey tribespeople turn to Christ in a great moving of God during 1963, and they are still turning!

Dinh Nai and his wife, a bright, attractive young couple, had been won to the Lord by the Vietnamese preacher, Mr. Khiem of Son Ha, and had two years' training in our Bible School at Da Nang. They always did well in their studies. They are Hrey tribespeople, but as children they received a little schooling and learned to read and write Vietnamese fluently. Their parents, on both sides, are intelligent and influential in their village of Ruong Khai and they and all the rest of their families also believed on Christ under Mr. Khiem's teaching. Nai and his pretty wife, Ngoi, have always been great favorites in their own village.

In September, 1962, the Field Committee placed this couple and their three children in the large re-settlement village of Ha Bak, with two more resettled villages nearby — their own home

village of Ruong Khai and Ha Thanh. These three villages are
in the thickly populated Son Ha District.

Nai began to witness for God in his native village of Ruong
Khai, and he immediately saw a moving of the Spirit of God
among the sorcerers there. They began to be discontented with
their old animal sacrifices and the offering of the blood and alcohol to the demons. They would come to Nai and ask him for
some of the good medicines our mission had given him for distribution. Nai wanted to make them really see how foolish are
their old superstitions and sacrifices to the demons. These sorcerers lead the whole village in following the devil. So he would
say to the sorcerers as they came to him:

"Oh, so you want medicine for a backache? Then why don't
you offer a sacrifice to the devil you call Bu Rai! He is the
backache expert!"

Or — "And you want medicine for fever? Then why don't you
sacrifice to your devil Bu Ha Van? You are a sorcerer — a spir-
itualist medium, aren't you?"

As Nai passed their sacrificial altars throughout the village, and
saw the sorcerers calling on the spirits, he'd laughingly tease them
saying, "Ah! You know you didn't tell the truth that time in that
incantation to the evil spirits, did you?" He was as bold as Elijah
of old, mocking the prophets of Baal.

The old sorcerers are so fond of young Nai that they would
laugh at his making fun of them and they took no offense at all.
He can get away with this joking about their false worship where
others, less sharp-witted and popular, couldn't.

He let them suffer for two or three months without helping
them with the medicines. He told them firmly that they must
truly give up all their foolish old animal sacrifices and witchcraft
and turn with all their hearts to the true God before he would
help them. This strategy worked and the sorcerers and people
really began to forsake their sacrifices.

It is a wonderful victory when a sorcerer will accept Christianity. It means that he gives up his authority in the village —
his hold over the ignorant. He will lose all the gifts of chickens,
goats, pigs, and cows that he formerly received in payment for his
witchcraft. So it is nothing short of a miracle when even *one*

sorcerer believes. But here were twenty-three sorcerers in two villages turning to the true God!

When he saw that they were sincere, Nai gave out the good medicines to them. With some of his own money he started buying some of the wonderful antibiotics on his own and treating the people. He saw some marvelous cures.

Medical assistance goes hand-in-hand with preaching the Gospel to these tribespeople. How many times have we found that new converts have back-slidden because they have become ill. As they had no medicine to help them, they were tempted to go back to their old heathen animal sacrifices and the offering of blood to appease the demons "who made them sick." A few pills can tide these poor people over this critical period, until their faith in the Lord is strong and sure and their hearts are changed and they will have no more desire to return to the old false, ignorant superstitions and sacrifices.

Hundreds of Hrey tribespeople at Ha Bak had just been brought back from the Communists in the mountains. They were hungry, had no clothing, and many were sick and dying. Nai and his wife took five of these miserable ones into their own little bamboo hut, fed them, gave them medicines and they were healed.

Nai saw to it that the sorcerers burnt up all their demon paraphernalia of chicken feathers, vertebrae of snakes, claws, tails of deer, heads of buffalo — all sorts of charms and rubbish. They were willing now to be done with it all. They began to realize that it was all lies of the devil. Light was dawning in their poor, dark hearts. After the burnings, they could come to Nai's little house where he held the meetings, and Nai would pray for them and lead them to pray and accept Christ, the Son of God, as their great Sacrifice. His sermons to them were on repenting of their sins; forsaking the demons; giving up the sacrifices and rice-alcohol and accepting Jesus Christ as their own Eternal Saviour. They had followed and served the devil for years. Now they must serve Jesus until they died.

As the people defied the evil spirits to follow Christ, they saw that no evil befell them! They began to feel so free from their old fears and the lies they had believed! They were transformed and smiles lit their faces!

Top: A Hrey longhouse in Ha Bak with new church building rising in background.
Left: Hrey girl in Ha Bak weaving cotton blanket.
Below: Resettled village of Ha Bak with new chapel in center background.

Top: Dr. and Mrs. Stuart Harverson, missionaries for 25 years.
Top right: Pastor Dinh Nai and
  his wife, Ngoi, and children.
Right: Dr. Harverson teaching
  Ha Bak Hrey young men to
  read and write their own language, and the rudiments of
  First Aid.
Below: Christmas party, 1963,
  at Ha Bak.

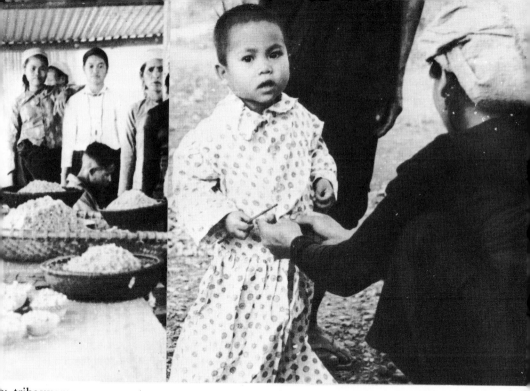

y tribeswomen prepare trays
oked rice for Christmas feast.

Hrey baby girl gets new dress for
Christmas.

The two little Hrey boys wait their
turn to wear some of the clothes
from America. It's 65 degrees but
there's not enough to go around.

Heading home by bicycle.

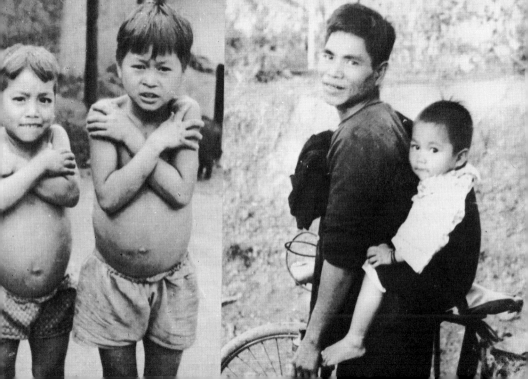

Early in 1963, Nai came in to Da Nang with his merry face bright and his black eyes sparkling, and told us that sixty Hreys had believed on Christ in Ruong Khai and Ha Bak.

The Bible Evangelistic car, with preachers Tri and Luong and others, went out to Ha Bak and ministered there for several days. Fifty more people made commitments to Christ under their ministry.

Then Nai came in with the joyful news that there were now in the two villages two hundred who believed. They gathered in the open outside of Nai's small bamboo house, standing sometimes for two hours or more for the meetings. Some of the former sorcerers could read a little Vietnamese, and so could read some of the Bible verses. They began to learn to pray and sing and recite Bible texts. They rejoiced in the meetings with Nai and didn't want to miss a single one.

Dr. and Mrs. Harverson, who had been working among the Hrey tribespeople at Bato, were away on furlough in Australia and New Zealand for six months. When they returned in April, 1963, they heard of this great turning of the Hreys to God in the villages of Ruong Khai and Ha Bak, and they were filled with joy.

Dr. Harverson felt the call of God to go out to camp in Ha Bak and help Nai and his wife shepherd this great flock in these villages. He drove out over the bad Dong Ke-Son Ha road in from the main coastal highway. It is full of deep holes and ruts. On a recent trip, the doctor's Land Rover was stuck three times. Once, the American officers pulled him out. The second time, a Vietnamese army truck got him free. The third time, some tribes soldiers pushed the Rover out of a terrible hole. He camped out there for two weeks at a time, then would return to Da Nang where Mrs. Harverson is living in part of one of our Mission houses for the time being. She is studying Vietnamese.

The doctor stays in Da Nang for just a few days getting some Hrey Bible Lessons mimeographed, then he goes back to Ha Bak again. He lives right in the poor little bamboo shack with Nai and eats the food Mrs. Nai cooks for them. Sometimes they have strange concoctions, like fish and pineapple boiled together. At other seasons it is pumpkin and fish — not so bad with red peppers. They eat tough, scrawny chicken and ducks and duck eggs.

The doctor is able to minister to hundreds of sick tribespeople.

His medicine and good professional care replace the hideous old superstitions and horrible practices of torturing and slaying poor animals and sprinkling their blood over doorposts, gongs, drums and the sick persons.

There is a terrifying amount of sickness through the valley — children with distended stomachs and rickety limbs; scaly eyes, with trachoma, is rife. There are ugly ulcers and much tuberculosis, with awful racking coughs. The doctor is treating forty T.B. patients regularly. The conditions in the crowded re-settled villages are terribly unsanitary, and there is appalling need on every hand. But Dr. Harverson is a seasoned missionary-doctor and he comes to grips with these diseases and prays the sick ones through to deliverance, as well as helping them with pills. He preaches the Gospel to each patient.

The Trebilcos at Bato have translated a little book of hymns into the Hrey language and now the doctor, Nai and his wife, use this and the people can sing many hymns now in their own tribal tongue. These hymns have been a great blessing in teaching clearly the way to heaven. Now the people love to sing in Hrey, "There is a Fountain Filled With Blood." Their favorites today are, "The Cleansing Stream I see, I see!" and "Come Ye Disconsolate — Earth has no sorrow that heaven cannot heal."

From twenty to thirty boys and girls come nearly every evening to sing — some from Ruong Khai, two miles away. Those from far away stay the night as they couldn't go back after ten o'clock curfew in this time of war. They all crowd into Nai's shack — eight or ten boys sleeping on one bed and others on chairs placed together. All are in the same room where Dr. Harverson has his narrow camp-cot. He hears them jabbering Hrey in their sleep.

The children sing well — even learning bass and tenor parts to some hymns! Today they know more than thirty hymns by heart and sing these gospel messages with real understanding.

Nai and Dr. Harverson began to plan for a church building for two hundred people. Nai and a good group of his Christian men collected the materials for building. By the time they had quite a lot of bamboo gathered in, there were three hundred people who had turned to Christ and were all attending the Sunday morning meetings outside of Nai's own hut. Many came from Ruong Khai and also a number were now turning to Christ in Ha Thanh village, three miles away in another direction.

With the help of the Native Church Crusade fund from Dallas, Texas, Nai and his Christians put up a nice chapel where three hundred people could squeeze in.

Gordon and I went out with Dr. Harverson for several days and had a joyous time seeing this great working of the Holy Spirit of God and this fine group of Christians in three villages being built up in the Lord. We joined in witnessing to them and showed them many Bible story flannelgraphs. We had big meetings each night until 10 P.M. curfew in front of Nai's house.

By the time the church building was finished, some months later, 400 older people gathered for the meetings, with as many more children. So the chapel was too small from the beginning. There are no walls at the sides or back — just up at the front — so as to make more room. On Sundays, when Nai preached, he had to stand up on a table on a raised piece of ground outside, at the back of the chapel and shout at the top of his lungs. Even so, he couldn't be heard clearly by all. The crowds were overflowing outside of the church and down the banks!

They will soon have chapels built at Ruong Khai and Ha Thanh and the big crowd won't all have to meet in Ha Bak.

How wonderful to hear them sing, "The Cleansing Wave" and "Earth has no sorrow that heaven cannot heal," instead of their old incantations and shrieking to the spirits and the thudding of gongs and drums calling on the demons. Now the whole village echoes with the songs of Zion. Witchcraft is losing its power in these three re-settlement villages. They are learning now of the One who loves them and who gave His Life as a great Sacrifice for them.

What joy to begin to see "the Kingdoms of this world becoming the Kingdoms of our Lord and of His Christ" in this Hrey area.

The Living Christ is at work through the Power of His Spirit. He is abundantly able to turn men from darkness to light and from the power of Satan unto God, if we will but make the effort and let Him use us, as the doctor and Nai are doing.

At the close of 1963, almost all of Ruong Khai village had

turned to Christ. There was hardly any sorcery left there. This is also true in Ha Bak. In Ha Thanh, thirty-five people accepted Christ in one week and the whole village shows promise of turning.

Nai and the doctor visit in the Son Ha center also. The road is still too dangerous with Communists to get into Gi Liang, where another Hrey evangelist, Tho, is working. In Son Ha, Nai wants to hold out on giving the medicine there, until the people make a clean break from their sorcery and sacrifices, to God. This strategy has worked well in the three re-settlement villages. So Nai is putting these Son Ha people to the same test. "It's no use helping them with a little medicine until they turn properly to God," he says. "If we do, they'll sacrifice animals as well, and they'll thank the devil for healing them. Let them make a clean break first and come through for God."

Each day in Ha Bak is very full for Dr. Harverson and Nai. A special gift from Australia was sent to the doctor for a Hrey Hospital. With this money God led him to take on five bright Hrey young men as students. The doctor is training them in medicine and the Word. They will make future leaders in these villages for the Lord. These five students spend all day long with the doctor and Nai. Two of them, until they came into the re-settlement village, had been living back in the jungle mountains with the Communists.

They arrive at 7:30 each morning and help the doctor with the morning clinic line-up until about 8:30. Then they all gather around a table for prayer, singing and study. The first step was for the doctor to introduce them to Hrey writing and Hrey booklets. The Trebilcos at Bato have translated a Hrey catechism, and some Bible stories, besides the hymn-book. The doctor is also teaching the students about the New Testament Church and the qualifications of elders and deacons.

Then they learn medical instruction and have such words as Streptomycin and Tetracyclin to learn to pronounce. They also treat patients during their study hours in medicine as part of their curriculum. The students practice on injecting bananas at first. Then the doctor invites them to practice on each other, but he says that "here they are backward in coming forward!"

At about 4:30 P.M. they all go out to visit the villages with

medicines and to pray for the sick for about two hours. Sometimes they go out again after supper, with a lantern — Communist
snipers notwithstanding!

They have recently translated "Am I a Soldier of the Cross?"
into Hrey and it is going over well. The Hrey word for "angel"
is much the same as for "soldier" — and Dr. Harverson was won-
dering why the students were referring to themselves as "angels"
when they prayed!

They are learning how to really pray. One morning, one of the
students, Droa, sixteen years old, was absent from class. The
buffaloes, belonging to his family, were all lost in the jungle. The
doctor and the students all had prayer about it and Droa found his
buffaloes unharmed. The following day, the same thing happened
with Rah's oxen!

The doctor asked all his students to write out in their note-
books the qualifications of a deacon. Jan, aged 24, wrote:

"I am a deacon. I have one wife. I keep my children in order.
I love my people and try to help them."

This is truly a working of the Holy Spirit of God in these villages. At Christmas time, 1963, there were 1,700 who came to
the Christmas feast — eating in relays in the chapel all morning.
The Christians themselves had given the buffalo meat and rice for
their food, and a dozen or so kind, friendly American soldiers in
a Special Forces Camp nearby gave them some pounds of candy.
For Christmas presents, there was some clothing sent from the
Mennonites in America — enough for two pieces of clothing to
each family, for such a large crowd. They take turns in wearing
the clothes, from the oldest to the youngest. All Christmas afternoon, Nai and the doctor held meetings.

Early in 1964, Nai now counts the number of Hrey who have
truly turned to Christ in this section as 1000! How we praise
the Lord! There will soon be a baptismal service when 50 or so
will be baptized — just those who have trusted and obeyed the
Lord for a number of months and who are following a high
standard of Christian living. They must be all-out for the Lord
and must have given up all tobacco and betel-nut chewing before
they can partake of this holy ceremony.

These villages are in a dangerous area. Just two miles away

from Ha Bak, the Vietnamese Army heard that there was a Communist training camp hidden in the jungle. In October, 1963, when a patrol went in to find the Camp, they were ambushed and two American advisors and a number of the Vietnamese and Hrey government soldiers were killed.

Dr. Harverson knows that he, especially because he is a valuable doctor, is a marked man by the Communists. But still he carries on. He knows that the lady doctor, Dr. Vietti, and two men missionaries, were captured by the Communists from the Banmethuot Leprosarium in May, 1962, and have not been heard from since.

But it is because of this noble missionary spirit that the tribes are finding Christ today.

▶ 26 ◀
"Happy Haven" Leprosarium Underway

THE TELEGRAM READ, "HALLELUJAH! Leprosarium land author-ized!" Mr. Nhut, the chairman of our National Church, had just signed the papers in Saigon and sent us the wire on January 4, 1964. Gordon and I broke down and wept for joy! At last our hope was realized! Our hearts became robust and jubilant! After over six years of frustration and almost blasted hopes, the govern-ment of Viet Nam had finally granted us a site for our "Happy Haven Leprosarium."

Now the seemingly insurmountable obstacles and impossibilities were overcome. We had government permission for the land on which to build our hospital and all the other buildings of a Leprosy Village. We could now obey God's command to "Go ye forth" to help these poor ones. When some of the buildings were up we could start to bring in these shunned outcasts. What a great privilege it would be to be able to help lift their burdens! Now they could have a nice home, kindly care, medical treatment and they would learn of Him who can indeed lift all their burdens.

With light, joyous hearts — because we love these poor people with leprosy so much and rejoice that we can help them — we have now plunged into the great task of constructing this leprosy settlement which will care for hundreds of neglected sufferers afflicted with this awful malady.

"Happy Haven Leprosarium" is being built on a large stretch of pale beige sand, half of which was already planted a few years ago with filao — the tropical, long-leafed pine trees. In three more

232

years they will become a lovely soughing forest. We have now planted one thousand coconut palms which will make the place very scenic. In sandy land we can also plant all types of acacia trees, like the gorgeous Flame of the Forest, to add to the beauty of the place.

There is a good road to Da Nang ten miles away and building materials are available close by. We have only to dig a few feet to get good water in wells. The cement brick hospital, with red-tiled roof, is built on a slight rise of ground giving a magnificent view of every point of the horizon — the distant limpid blues of mountain ranges in the west and the fantastic Marble Mountains of Da Nang close by, that rise straight up out of the sandy desert. They are beautiful phantom rocks and caves of pink, gray and white marble. The sparkling blue South China Sea is just a few hundred yards in the foreground. From the standpoint of security, in this time of war, it should be safe as all this section is well guarded. We want to make it a garden of comfort for these, who through no fault of their own, have had to "walk alone" in suffering and mental agony for so long.

While the sandy soil is the main disadvantage to making the settlement self-supporting, they can grow sweet potatoes, and possibly a few other things, like beans and peanuts, in the wet season with good fertilizers. The main advantages are the healthful climate, with sea breezes; the isolation from villages; the easy accessibility; and the spaciousness, with lots of room for expansion. The patients who are able, can go deep-sea fishing, raise chickens, ducks and rabbits and fish in ponds; and there will be facilities for vocational training later on.

The psychological effect of the new, clean, happy surroundings is wonderful. The patients are well-looked after with our native nurse, Mr. Toi, and our English missionary, John Haywood, in charge. About one mile away, we have a good group of Christian fishermen won to the Lord over a year ago, with a fine Vietnamese pastor, Mr. Luong, who cares for this flock. He now visits the leprosy patients frequently and comes every Sunday to give them a good service, until they will have their own pastor at the close of our Bible School in May, when we'll have more student preachers to allocate.

Top: Leprosy patients taking a load of sprouted coconuts to be planted
   at Happy Haven.
Below: Happy Haven patients happily planting sprouted coconuts.

When we began this construction, we had funds on hand for a modest hospital and a ward, a dormitory and the water system. Some of our Bana leprosy rehabilitation patients were brought in to make thousands of cement blocks and to make roads and buildings. The hospital houses our new portable X-Ray machine, which was also given by U.S.O.M. through the Health Department.

One of our great concerns will be to segregate the untainted children from their infected parents in a nursery of their own, in a section where the healthy personnel live. Their relatives can often see them there but will not be in direct contact with them, for this means almost certain infection. One of the basic problems of leprosy is the prevention of the disease in children. Leprosy is a disease of children. It is estimated that 75% of the adults who have leprosy today contracted it before adolescence.

We must detect and treat early cases, for these can be cured with the sulphones. Another nursery and children's home will have to be built for those little ones who already have leprosy and have no parents to care for them.

We especially want to bring in the tribespeople from the mountains who have no care whatever. They are not permitted in the fortified zones. We think of the people with leprosy that we just recently saw at Ha Bak, outside of the re-settlement villages — living in dog-kennel thatched huts, with scarcely room for one person to sleep in, curled up. They have been wasting away in terrible disfigurement, as they have anxiously awaited our Haven of Hope.

The Health Department of the Government of Viet Nam has promised their help and will give us more equipment, through U. S. Aid. The Mennonite Central Committee will continue to give us relief food for the patients, such as corn meal, bulgar (specially prepared) wheat, cheese, salad oil. They are giving us wheat flour now which is made into bread for the patients by Chinese bakers each day. The Government Social Service Department will give us a few cents each day per patient toward their food requirements.

For many years the Government Health Department has given us certain simple medicines for our various stations, and they will increase this aid to include special help to the Leprosarium, including the sulphone drugs for leprosy. We already have a great stock of bandages on hand sent by kind friends in the homelands.

Besides our present missionary and national medical staff we need the following foreign personnel:

1.) *Physio-therapist.* To help in the important work of rehabilitating hands and feet, to help them avoid being crippled.

2.) *Orthopedic surgeon.* To rehabilitate hands, feet and faces by surgery, in order that patients may do useful work and have less stigma when they re-enter society. This includes new eyebrows, noses, as well as making it possible for them to use hands and feet that were badly crippled.

3.) *Nurses.* Missionary nurses are needed to oversee and train national nurses, most of whom will be patients, and to train laboratory technicians and pharmacists.

We are praying that God will send us truly devoted and well-trained workers who will have a special, tender love for our people with leprosy. Missionaries who will heed God's call and respond gladly with great compassion to help those who bear the heaviest burdens of all — these are the ones we covet.

So we are forging ahead now in this wonderful job of building a Happy Haven for the hundreds of suffering Vietnamese and tribespeople. You should see the joy on their faces as we kneel down with them — with their ulcered, toeless feet and awful bodies — to pray to our Saviour.

"Is there no balm in Gilead?

Is there no Physician there?"

"Yes — There is a Balm in Gilead, to make the wounded whole.
There is a Balm in Gilead to heal the sin-sick soul."

"The Great Physician now is near, the sympathizing Jesus;
He speaks the drooping heart to cheer,
Oh, hear the Voice of Jesus!"

Their sorrows bring them near to God. They are down in the valley of pain and they rejoice to turn to the Lord who cares for them, loves them and who suffered and died to save them. Truly He is their Great Physician who restores their souls.

▶ 27 ◀

Keeping Up the Pace

STILL THE NEW HORIZONS stretch out ahead of us — ever beckoning, ever challenging.

With the change of government in Viet Nam on November 1, 1963, everyone's hopes for the future were strengthened. Now a new day appears to be dawning in Viet Nam with the prospect of political stability being established. The fight against the Communists is being pressed with increasing vigor and the final victory is being brought much closer. With the overthrow of the old government regime and its abuses, we are hoping that the people will be less fearful of following the Lord Jesus Christ. We look forward to even greater religious freedom. If we are to believe the spirit of the new government, it will mean that mission matters will be expedited, authorizations for land and churches should be granted more speedily. We have already seen this come to pass in the matter of our new leprosarium site.

The prospect looks bright that this sorely distressed land will enjoy peace and stability in the not-too-distant future.

We are still in the front line of battle against the Communists. We are never without sharp reminders of this, even here in the well-protected city of Da Nang — the sound of guns, the droning of planes all day long, the rushing of armies, the dead and wounded soldiers brought in to the city hospital by helicopters, and hundreds of American advisors all over the town.

Out in the country, the villages everywhere are turned into fortresses, there are night curfews, challenging sentries, rumors, alarms and all the sorrows of war. There is still much unrest, danger and bloodshed.

Top: Group of Vietnamese girls singing Christmas music at Kontum.
Below: Closing day exercises of Bible School, April 30, 1963.

Top: Students and teachers of the Bible School at Da Nang.
Below: Senior class in Bible School which studied the book of Ephesians under Mrs. Smith's guidance.

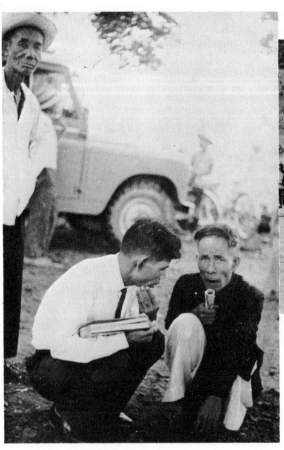

Top: The Bible Evangelistic car and Team in resettlement village near Dak Pek.

Left: Preacher Luong, with the Bible Evangelistic car, talks with an older Vietnamese man concerning spiritual truths.

Below: The house of the Spraggett's, Roy and Daphne and baby Jenny, after it was blown up by the communists. The family is now recuperating in a London hospital.

We must keep training the national workers for God in our Bible Schools. They can go back to their own people and say, "See, we have given up all of these old superstitions and horrible heathen customs" — such as the terrible cutting out of the children's teeth and the cruel animal sacrifices among the tribespeople.

Christianity is the only religion that can raise up Viet Nam. The false faiths of Buddhism, Confucianism, Taoism, Cao Daiism, Animism and the tribal animal sacrifices, cannot save these people! Only Christ can help them. The responsibility rests with us Christians to bring Christ to them, who lifts them out of ignorance, superstition, magic and sorcery. Of what magnitude is the task of the missionaries to make Him known! You helpers in the homelands fight side by side with us. "Is anything too hard for the Lord?" The power of the Gospel can cope with the lowest forms of heathenism and the worst phases of superstition. Oh, the power of just the simple preaching of the Gospel, and the Word of God, and the gospel songs!

We are only a small handful of missionaries out here to evangelize all these multitudes in ignorance and darkness. Seven years ago this mission was just a little seed with two workers. Today we have seventeen stout-hearted foreign missionaries, forty-seven national evangelists, and twenty-five mission stations. But we must have many scores more of missionaries and mission-stations that the Father may be glorified. We need heroes and heroines for Christ as re-enforcements. We want to see these new ones coming — fresh, eager, dynamic, audacious for Christ and Viet Nam — who will laugh off dangers and discomforts. They will be given the honor of being among the first to go as brethren to these backward members of the human family, to point them to Jesus, the Saviour of all mankind.

The multitudes are waiting for the workers. Will the workers come? Or will these piteous throngs go on waiting until it is too late, and they cry out as they go into eternity, "The harvest is past, and we are not saved!"?

WAGGONER CHRISTIAN CHURCH

Epilogue

IT WAS A QUIET NIGHT up at Cam Phu where Daphne and Roy Spraggett, with their little two-year-old daughter, Jennifer, were stationed among the Baru tribespeople. There was an armed Vietnamese guard of fourteen men stationed within a forty-yard radius of their little home, watching over the hamlet of Cam Phu.

Around 4:15 A.M. Jenny became fussy and Daphne got up and took the baby into bed with her. It was just a few minutes later that a tremendous explosion blew their house to bits! The Communists had placed a mine right inside their bathroom, next to their bedroom wall! A long wire led out from the bomb into a nearby field and the Communists had set off the bomb from out there. The Vietnamese guards were asleep. The walls of the house fell in and the roof of fibro-cement sheeting blew off! If Jenny had been in her little bed by the wall she would have been crushed to death. All three Spraggetts were stunned unconscious. Daphne came to first and she was standing up. She thought she was having a nightmare! Then she realized that their house was a terrible shambles and they were surrounded by fire!

The kerosene heater in their bedroom had exploded with the bomb, spewing flames all over the place. Jenny was still on Daphne's bed. When Daphne saw Roy she thought he was dead! His feet and legs were still on his bed which was burning, and they were covered with heavy rubble. His body and head were twisted on the floor and his face was a mass of blood. Daphne quickly moved Jenny out of danger of the fire and then she tried to pull the heavy rubble off of Roy's legs, but she couldn't in her own wounded condition.

242

The Vietnamese evangelist and his wife, Mr. and Mrs. Huan, sleeping in the little chapel next door, came running and the civil guards arrived. Some of the women took Daphne and the baby over to the preacher's house while the men moved Roy. The hamlet chief radioed the district and province chiefs and the native preacher and his wife gave all the first aid they could. All this time Roy remained unconscious.

At daybreak the ambulance arrived and took the Spraggetts to Quang Tri where an American Army major, a doctor and other American military men met them. They did what was immediately essential for the Spraggetts, then put them into a helicopter and flew them to Hue. There, a special American plane was waiting to fly them to the American Army Hospital in Nha Trang, 600 miles down the coast. Our mission doctor, Dr. Harverson, in Da Nang, immediately followed them to Nha Trang in another plane.

In the hospital, Roy and Daphne quickly underwent surgery to get out some of the shrapnel. Roy's left shoulder blade and clavicle were broken and his head and face were wounded. He had extensive burns from his hips downward, especially bad on both of his feet. Jenny had burns and cuts on her little body. Daphne's left heel was broken and she had other wounds in her feet. The doctor removed a door hinge and screws from her heel, and later on, still more screws imbedded in the bones had to be taken out! She, too, had head and face wounds, and all three were suffering deafness in both ears from the terrible explosion.

Gordon and I flew to Saigon to meet the Spraggetts when they were flown there from Nha Trang one week later. They were brought on stretchers on a big C-123 freighter plane and an American ambulance was at the plane door to take them to one of the best Saigon hospitals. We wept as we saw them — their feet and legs in casts and Roy's shoulder and arm also in a cast, with the arm stretched upward. The plane trip had been rough on them and Roy cried, "Oh, Laura and Gordon, we've had an awful beating up!" But they were as cheery and brave as their sufferings would allow.

They received good care for ten days in the air-conditioned

The Spraggetts are dearly loved by the tribespeople and the Vietnamese, and the attack upon their lives was a great shock to all their friends.

Saigon Hospital, but facilities for proper treatment for them were lacking. British Embassy friends in Saigon were most generous and kind to them.

The Pan American Airways fixed up a place especially for them on a regular jet to London, with a stretcher and curtains for Roy, and Daphne lay on three seats. Altogether they took up the space of twelve seats but the airline only charged for three places. Baby Jennifer wasn't wounded as badly as her parents and she recuperated quickly from her burns. Pamela Brady, the English missionary nurse, whose furlough was due at this time, accompanied them home to London. They have been placed in a splendid hospital there and are now receiving the best of care. They will have to rest many months before their wounds are all healed. Roy will be permanently deaf in his left ear.

They are eager to return here to their beloved field of service in Viet Nam, as soon as the doctors say they are fit. Their house and nearly all of their belongings have been destroyed. They are paying the price to get the Gospel to the Baru.

Just before the explosion, Roy had written an article in the W. E. C. magazine, "World-Wide," telling of three Baru Christian tribesmen, Yong, Oai and Tanang, who have been snatched away from their villages near Cam Phu by the Communists and are now in terrible dungeons, or most likely, have been killed. Roy wrote, "They have been counted worthy to suffer for Christ and will enjoy the Saviour's reward. The challenge comes to us: *Can we match their sacrifice?* Will we let atheistic Communism swallow up the 400,000 tribespeople of Central Viet Nam and the millions of Vietnamese people here, while we casually sing, 'The Whole Wide-World for Jesus!' No! We must match sacrifice with sacrifice!"

The Spraggetts were indeed called upon "to match the sacrifice" of their three fellow Christians, the Baru tribesmen. They count it a privilege to have been given this mark of closer identification with them.

The Spraggets had been doing a fine work among the Baru — speaking the tribal language fluently, preaching in the strategic hamlet villages and ministering a great deal to the sick. They were helping to make the Strategic Hamlet program a success in the Cam Phu area and this was hindering the Communists in their great desire to destroy this hamlet program.

Can we, too, "match their sacrifice"?

266.0235
S6542

LINCOLN CHRISTIAN COLLEGE AND SEMINARY

11934

WAGGONER CHRISTIAN CHURCH

WAGGONER CHRISTIAN CHURCH

3 4711 00182 3717

266.0235 S6542
Smith, Laura Irene Ivory.
Victory in Viet Nam

DEMCO